EMILE DURKHEIM

KENNETH THOMPSON, B. A., D. Phil.
Reader in Sociology
The Open University, Milton Keynes

ELLIS HORWOOD LIMITED
Publishers · Chichester

TAVISTOCK PUBLICATIONS
London and New York

First published in 1982 by
ELLIS HORWOOD LIMITED
Market Cross House, Cooper Street
Chichester, Sussex, PO19 1EB, England
and

TAVISTOCK PUBLICATIONS LIMITED
11 New Fetter Lane, London EC4P 4EE

Published in the USA by
TAVISTOCK PUBLICATIONS
and ELLIS HORWOOD LIMITED
in association with METHUEN INC.
733 Third Avenue, New York, NY 10017

© 1982 K. Thompson/Ellis Horwood Ltd.

British Library Cataloguing in Publication Data
Thompson, Kenneth
Emile Durkheim.
1. Durkheim — Emile — Criticism and interpretation
I. Title
301'.092'4   HM22.F8D8/

Library of Congress Card No. 81-20294 AACR2

ISBN 0-85312-394-2 (Ellis Horwood Ltd. — Library Edn.)
ISBN 0-85312-419-1 (Ellis Horwood Ltd. — Student Edn.)

Typeset in Press Roman by Ellis Horwood Ltd.
Printed in Great Britain by R. J. Acford, Chichester.

Table of Contents

KENNETH THOMPSON is Reader in Sociology at
the Open University, Milton Keynes. He graduated
from the University of Leicester in 1963 with a
B.A. in Social Sciences, and was awarded a D.Phil.
in Sociology in 1967 by the University of Oxford.

He was assistant Professor of Rutgers University,
New Jersey, USA, from 1967 to 1968, and at Smith
College, Massachusetts, USA, from 1968 to 1970.
He took up his present position in 1970, returning
to Smith College as a visiting Professor for the year
1980-81.

His publications include works on the subjects of:
Bureaucracy and Church Reform (1970), *Auguste
Comte: The Foundation of Sociology* (1976),
Sociological Perspectives (1971), *People and
Organisations* (1973), *Control and Ideology in
Organizations* (1980) and *An Introduction to
Sociology* (1980).

Foreword

Durkheim's claim to be a *key sociologist* must be a strong one. He stands along with Karl Marx and Max Weber — who also appear as subjects for books in this series — at the threshold of modern sociology. Durkheim devoted his life to the work of founding and building a professional sociology in France. He established University departments and learned societies, trained students in the theories and methods of the new science, and directed the publication of a journal (called *L'Année sociologique*) which was the mouthpiece of the sociological movement. In it the new sociologists could set out their ideas and list the results of their researches, and of course communicate with all those who took an interest in this new branch of human knowledge.

But Durkheim's indefatigable work in the organisation and institutional development of the delicate infant sociology is not, by and large, what he is best known for. Four major studies have assured him a place in the history of sociology's intellectual development: *The Division of Labour in Society* (1893); *The Rules of Sociological Method* (1895); *Suicide* (1897) and *The Elementary Forms of the Religious Life* (1912).

These books alone were enough to assure his fame, but when set along-side his patient work in coaxing the French educational system to take sociology seriously, we are able to make out the true image of a man who was totally dedicated to his science. He provided sociology in France with both the institutional context and the theories and methods which assured its survival, and made of it something which excited scholars and thinkers in other countries. His methods and concepts were rapidly taken up, especially in the USA and Britain where nascent sociologists were emerging. But his influence was not only felt where sociology was growing. The uses to which his ideas were put make him a key figure in fields outside of academic sociology. His extensive work on the sources of social cohesion proved to be of interest to industrial sociologists and industrial relations experts, who used it to increase productivity whilst at the same time making many repetitive manual and clerical jobs less boring.

In the academic world, his influence on the discipline of anthro-pology and history was decisive in their movement towards the use of sociological conceptions of their subject matter and methods. The so-called 'structuralism' of the French anthropological school, exempli-fied at its most impressive by the writings of Claude Lévi-Strauss, owes a great deal to the work of Durkheim and his followers like Mauss, Granet and Lévy-Bruhl, British anthropology was also heavily influenced by the approaches adopted by the Durkheimians. History too has felt the impact of methods and ideas which originated with Durkheim. The immensely influential *Annales* school of historians, who are largely responsible for the fact that modern history is more concerned with the features of everyday life in the epochs which it studies than with the doings of 'great men', was built on foundations erected by Durkheim. Such writers as Bloch and Febvre in the early days of the Annales group, and more recently Braudel, Duby and Le Roy Ladurie (of *Montaillou* fame) took much of their inspiration from the intellecutal drive of *l'Année sociologique*.

There can be little doubt that Durkheim's theories and methods have provided the grounding of a considerable portion of modern sociology. And yet, like all key figures his work is capable of many 'readings', some of which have led to uses which he would not always have thought to be correct extensions of his principles. In this book Kenneth Thompson looks at what Durkheim wrote, presenting it to us in the light of both its original context and the very widely varying ways in which subsequent writers and thinkers across a range of disci-plines have used it. As he points out, Durkheim succeeded in giving to sociology its 'academic credibility and influence' at a time when his illustrious forebear, Auguste Comte, had set the infant science an ambitious prospectus and given it a name but very little else. It could have gone the way of many fanciful Victorian projects. The fact that it did not is due in large part to the genius and diligence of Émile Durkheim. Kenneth Thompson explores the genius of Durkheim in this book, but at the same time shows its context and its limits.

"To add a science to the list of sciences is always a very laborious operation, but more productive than the annexation of a new continent to old continents. And it is at once much more fruitful when the science has man for its object. It almost had to do violence to the human spirit and to triumph over the keenest resistance to make it understood that in order to act upon things it was first necessary to put them on trial. The resistance has been particularly stubborn when the material to be examined was ourselves, due to our tendency to place ourselves outside of things, to demand a place apart in the universe."

(Durkheim, 1962, pp. 142-3)

For Margaret and Clare

1

Introduction

1.1 INTRODUCTION

There are many versions of the history of sociology, but most concur in placing its birth in nineteenth century France. Claude Lévi-Strauss, writing in exile in America at the end of the Second World War, may have been exaggerating only slightly when he said that modern sociology was born for the purpose of rebuilding French society after the destruction wrought by the French Revolution of 1789 and the Prussian War of 1870-71. The two Frenchmen who did most to create the discipline were Auguste Comte (1798-1857) in the aftermath of the Revolution, and Émile Durkheim (1858-1917) after the Franco-Prussian War. Comte gave the subject its name and an ambitious prospectus; Durkheim gave it academic credibility and influence.

Despite its early birth, or because of it, sociology in France took a long time before it grew to anything remotely resembling the stature Comte predicted for it. Indeed, just as the British economy is said to have suffered from being the first to industrialize, so too French sociology was reckoned to have paid the price for its early birth. As

Lévi-Strauss said, it suffered from the gap which existed, at the time of its birth, between the boldness of its theoretical premonitions and the lack of concrete data: "Comte's sociology remained in suspense between its overwhelming ambitions and the frailty of its positive basis"[1].

One reason why Comte's sociology remained in suspense until Durkheim's time was that it awaited the outcome of the see-sawing balance of political forces in France that was not stabilized until late in the nineteenth century. For the hundred years that followed the Revolution of 1789 the society seemed to be in constant danger of swinging violently from revolution to dictatorship and back again. It was an external stimulus that precipitated a resolution of that uncertainty — France's disastrous defeat in the Franco–Prussian War. After that experience there was a steady rise to ascendancy of the forces in France that advocated "modernization" based on science and secular republican principles. Only on that basis, it was thought, could France be strenghtened and unified to compete with Germany.

Durkheim was better placed than most to have learned that lesson and to profit from it. He was born in Epinal, near the German border, and his town was occupied by German troops during the war when he was twelve. He was also Jewish, and the defeat led to an outbreak of scapegoating antisemitism. Later, in the 1890s, when there was another outbreak of antisemitism surrounding the Dreyfus affair, Durkheim wrote recollecting his experience at close quarters of the way in which Jews had been blamed for defeats [2]. In view of those experiences it is not surprising that he should have put his faith in social science as the best means of combating irrational prejudices, reactionary privileges and customs, and as a source of national and rational unity.

The circumstances and character of Durkheim's own education also fitted him to execute his mission of giving substance to the claims that Comte had made for sociology. Teachers such as Foustel de Coulanges and Émile Boutroux at the École Normale Supérieure introduced him to systematic empirical research and the comparative method, and taught him a philosophy of science that made sense of Comte's assertion that sociology could have a legitimate subject-matter of its own. The liberal republicans who eventually rose to power in the Third Republic after the Prussian War, many of whom were ex-Normaliens, encouraged Durkheim in his mission. One such was Louis Liard, the Director of Higher Education, who sent Durkheim to Germany in 1885–86, with the special mission of reporting on the social sciences in Germany and of making recommendations that could be acted on in reforming and expanding French education [3]. Within a few years Durkheim and Durkheimian sociology were powers in the land, from the Sorbonne in

Paris to the lycées of the most distant provinces. The village school-master, himself schooled in Durkheim's sociological method, was to be found propagating sociology as an alternative to the preaching of the Catholic priest. Comte's dream seemed to have been fulfilled. It was somewhat clouded by the First World War, in which many of Durkheim's young collaborators, including his son, were killed. Durkheim never recovered from that setback and died shortly afterwards; there was a terrible irony in the fact that French sociology, which had been brought to maturity by the German challenge, should in turn be decimated by it. A full recovery did not take place until after the Second World War, but its survival was helped by the fact that Durkheim's influence had spread to other disciplines, such as History, and to sociology abroad.

Another way of explaining the success of Durkheim's sociology is to analyse it as a class phenomenon, along Marxist lines. It would be something of an exaggeration to say that sociology grew up in a "debate with Marx's ghost", in view of the fact that Durkheim did not regard Marxism as a scientific competitor for sociology, but rather as a sympton of the troubled state of society [4]. Durkheim was certainly not engaged in an ideological conflict with intellectual Marxism. And his engagement with socialism, as we will see later, was complex and sympathetic. There is more truth in the observation that educational patronage and ideological affinity and usefulness to the ascendent political and class faction helped to establish Durkheimian sociology in France. Even so, it would be cynical and inaccurate to elevate political opportuneness to the rank of main causal factor in explaining Durkheim's success. Two other sorts of factors were at least as important. The first sort might be loosely termed "organizational" factors. They relate to Durkheim's abilities as leader of an intellecutal school, particularly his achievement in founding a superb scholarly journal, recruiting and knitting together a group of talented contributors, and drawing up programmatic statements that shaped the development of sociology in France and abroad. Secondly, and perhaps the most important factor in his success, there was the effectiveness of his own works in demonstating that he had developed an adaptable analytical method capable of being used in a wide variety of subject-areas.

Durkheim's programme for sociology began to emerge in his very first publications, which were book reviews in the *Revue philosophique*, in 1885. Once again it is clear that the German challenge and example provided a major spur. In a review of Ludwig Gumplowicz's *Grundriss der Soziologie* (Outline of Sociology) Durkheim lamented "how regrettable" it was that sociology, though French in origin, "should be so little known and so little followed in France", and that it was becoming "more and more a German science"[5]. In his first publication, a review of A. Schäffle, *Bau und Leben des sozialen Körpers* (Structure and Life of the Social Organism) [6], he praised those points that agreed with his own conception of sociology: the use of empirical methods to study social phenomena; sensitivity to the infinite complexity of the facts; the epistemological independence of sociology from biology; and an insistence on the specific reality of society as more than the sum of its parts, as a "real thing", analogous to an organism. Where he disagreed with Schäffle, and with a predecessor like Herbert Spencer and his successors in American sociology, was over the relationship between the individual and society. Schäffle appealed to individual reason as the basis for social consensus and social cohesion. For Durkheim, as a social realist, any emphasis on individual reason and will was unsociological and unrealistic. Sociology, by his definition, was about social structuring and structural determinism. It was in this structuring, as for example in language, that Durkheim found the social facts that constituted the real subject-matter of sociology. As he put it in the review of Schäffle:

> "There exists a social consciousness of which individual consciousnesses are, at least in part, only an emanation. How many ideas or sentiments are there which we obtain completely on our own? Very few. Each of us speaks a language which he has not himself created: we find it ready-made"[7].

But it was not true, as some critics alleged, that Durkheim's social realism and structuralism entailed a notion of a metaphysical "group mind". He was talking about an interpenetration of individual consciousnesses by an exchange of symbols:

> "But how are we to conceive of this social consciousness? Is it a simple and transcendent being, soaring above society? The metaphysician is free to imagine such an indivisible essence deep within all things! It is certain that experience shows us nothing of the sort. The collective mind (*l'esprit collectif*) is only a composite of individual minds. But the latter are not mechanically juxtaposed and closed off from another. They are in perpetual interaction through the exchange of symbols; they interpenetrate one another. They group themselves according to thier natural affinities; they co-ordinate and systematize themselves"[8].

This conception of consciousness structured by symbolic exchanges was elaborated at length with regard to phenomena such as religion and kinship in the later work of Durkheim and his nephew Marcel Mauss, and it formed the basis of the structuralist method made famous by Claude Lévi-Strauss. From an early stage Durkheim had this idea of developing a structuralist method which would penetrate and interrelate successive layers of the total social phenomenon. He envisaged a multi-layered model in which the most accessible surface layers of structure constituted a social substratum made up of material and organizational factors, such as geography, population, communication and transport facilities, architecture, group distribution and organization. But in being scientific, sociology would not stop at these surface layers, but go beneath them to disclose their relations with a deeper layer of social forces — "impersonal norms of thought and action that pre-eminently constitute the sociological phenomenon"[9]. It was a method that had been used unconsciously by some historians, said Durkheim, but it was the task of sociology to develop it and re-apply it in historical research:

> "Instead of stopping at the exclusive consideration of events that lie at the surface of social life, there has arisen the need for studying the less obvious points at the base of it — internal causes and impersonal, hidden forces that move individuals and collectivities. A tendency to this sort of study has already been manifested by some historians; but it is up to sociology to increase consciousness of it, to illuminate and develop it"[10].

As a result of his closer acquaintance with German social thought, gained during his visit there in 1886, Durkheim was able to clarify his view of the basic articulation of these structured layers. In some respects it was similar to Marx's structuralism, although Durkheim explicitly rejected contemporary charges that his sociology was little different from the "materialism" and "economic determinism" of Marx. He did admit that he had been introduced to Marx's thought during his stay in Germany, but he said that he had already formed his main conceptions before this point [12]. However, on certain matters, and when he thought the evidence warranted it, Durkheim's analysis was similar to that of Marx. For example, a core dynamic in Durkheim's theory on a topic like that treated in *The Division of Labour in Society,* involved the crystallization of patterns of social relations under pressure from the environment, and the succeeding crystallization of moral and cognitive categories and norms from these patterned social relationships. The casual flow was from material substratum (for example, population density and density of interaction) via group structure (for example, increased division of labour) to beliefs and norms (for example, the cult of the individual and contractual law). However, in addition to differing on many specifics, such as the importance of class conflict, Durkheim was much more insistent that causal connections ran in both directions between material substratum and mental phenomena. His objection to what he saw as Marx's economic determinism was that it was unscientific in assuming that certain factors had causal pre-eminence when that could only be a hypothesis. Causal relationships between different layers of social phenomena could only be established by empirical investigation in each specific case [13].

Durkheim's ideas did not develop in association with political activity. He had little taste for what he called *"la cuisine politique"*, the world of day to day politics. He was concerned about politics in the sense of long-term social trends and the moral bases of social action. But he believed such matters should not be left to political dogma and trials of strength. The vocation of sociology was to subject these matters to empirical investigation. That activity could best be carried on in institutions devoted to scholarship and the results disseminated through scholarly publications. In addition to establishing sociology as a university discipline, he secured wider influence for it through the journal he founded, *L'Année sociologique*. In fact, it was more than just a means of disseminating ideas. It functioned as Durkheim's version of the research institutes he had seen and admired in his investigation of German social sciences. From its first appearance in 1898, the journal was used as a means for building up sociology in a number of ways. It drew in specialists from other disciplines as well as promoting a high level of competence within the main topic areas of sociology as mapped out by Durkheim. Specialist work was integrated within the master scheme and by encouraging the use of a common methodology; this was aided by the fact that Durkheim himself wrote approximately 25% of the articles published during his lifetime, and a further 25% were by his two closest disciples, Bouglé and Mauss [14]. As well as publishing original articles on key sociological topics, the journal also provided secondary analyses of published material on such varied topics as French industrial plants, Bavarian peasant villages, Australian tribes, New York slum dwellers, and Sicilian criminals [15]. The international dimension was added to the journal's interdisciplinary outreach by virtue of the large number of foreign language publications reviewed. The awe which it inspired abroad, especially in countries where sociology was more amateurish, was testified to by its opposite number in Britain, the *Sociological Review*. In an article published shortly after Durkheim's death, the secretary of the Sociological Society in England proclaimed Durkheim the "leading sociologist of the world" and spoke of *l'Année sociologique* as "his most notable service to sociology"[16]. And while the *American Journal of Sociology* came close to portraying the Sociological Society in London as a faintly amusing gentlemen's club, its reviews of *l'Année sociologique* were more respectful, although marked by rivalry and disagreement [17].

One of the main intentions of this book is to correct the popular misconception of Durkheim as the founder of an ahistorical, conservative theory of society which came into its own in the expansionist period of American sociology after the Second World War. We will argue that his legacy is to be found much more widely dispersed, and that he did more to inculate a sociological perspective across the spectrum of academic disciplines than any other figure, with the possible exception of Marx. This contention has been substantiated most strongly in the case of the discipline of history.

Durkheim devoted much of his preface in the first issue of *l'Année sociologique* to the subject of the relations between sociology and history. He admitted that, in the past, sociology had not appealed to historians because of "the too general character of our theories and their inadequate documentation"[18]. He said he was thinking of the kind of sociological generalizations promulgated by August Comte and Herbert Spencer. Historians in turn had failed to be scientific in not adopting a systematic, comparative method, and in failing to analyse phenomena in structural terms. He quoted his old teacher in support of his belief in the necessary interdependence of the two disciplines: "Fustel de Coulanges was fond of repeating that true sociology is history: nothing is more incontestable provided that history is carried on sociologically"[19].

According to Durkheim, the kind of history that was not of interest to sociology had the role of individuals (kings, generals, statesmen, and so on) as its chief object, or which simply retraced in their chronological order a sequence of events (dynasties, wars, negotiations, and parliamentary events). This was precisely the kind of history being written in France until the adoption of a structuralist method transformed it, partly under the inspiration of Durkheimian sociology.

The transformation was brought about by the historians Marc Bloch and Lucien Febvre, who founded the journal *Annales: Economies, sociétés, civilisations,* in 1929, giving rise to the famous Annales School. Bloch and Febvre admitted that they had been inspired by Durkheim and *l'Année sociologique* [20]. And one of the most distinguished subsequent exponents of the Annales approach, Fernand Braudel, testified to the Durkheimian influence by saying that "long after the ancient thrust of Auguste Comte (1798-1857), a militant and almost completely new sociology rose like a sun in France with Emile Durkheim (1858-1917), and the review he founded in 1897 — the quickly famous *Année sociologique,* which became a favourite reading matter for an entire generation of young historians, from Lucien Febvre to Marc Bloch, André Piganiol, and Louis Gernet"[21].

Braudel's own monumental work, *The Mediterranean and the Mediterranean World in the Age of Philip II,* was a perfect example of Durkheimian sociological history. It traced the interrelation of different historical-temporal structures on several levels of the total social phenomenon that constituted Mediterranean society over a half century period. He sought to capture structures of change of different durations, and their intersection, involving factors ranging from geography to organizations and "mentalities".

Another example of the true Durkheimian heritage is to be found in the fusion of *Annales* history with rural sociology and anthropology in France. It has excited world-wide admiration and attempted emulation, and its attractiveness lies in the way in which it discloses the interrelationships of the different structural layers in a vivid way:

"For many historians and cultural anthropologists, the most rewarding aspect of the French approach to the rural world has been the recreation of a vivid and concrete human existence; not merely the formal design of the fields, the state of technology, the production and distribution of the fruits of the land, and the juridical framework that accompanied economic activities but also the attitudes and values — *moeurs* and *mentalities* — of ordinary people in a preindustrial society"[22].

Durkheim resisted the tendency for structuralism to lead to a dull formalism, which over-emphasized the static and unchanging abstractions. It was for this reason that he criticized Georg Simmel's idea of formal sociology, which seemed to represent a rival view of the subject, emanating again from Germany. Durkheim opposed Simmel's view and set out his reasons in a programmatic statement on "Sociology and its Scientific Field", which he published in the new Italian journal, *Rivista italiana di sociologia,* in 1900. He insisted that the structural method should relate not simply to external forms of association, but also to the material and intellectual content of collectivities. Furthermore, although the search for structure presumed a certain degree of stability in social phenomena, it had to be borne in mind that structures were dynamic and emerging:

"Structure itself is encountered in *becoming,* and one cannot illustrate it except by pursuing this process of becoming. It forms and dissolves continually; it is life arrived at a certain measure of consolidation; to disconnect it from the life from which it derives or from that which it determines is equivalent to dissociating things that are inseparable"[23].

It will be important to keep in mind this emphasis on history and the emergent character of structure when we consider the other major version of Durkheim's structuralism which, under the asuspices of Lévi-Strauss, has spread its influence beyond the social sciences and history and into cultural studies of all kinds. This type of structuralist analysis is more concerned with "invariance". Taking as its subject-matter underlying codes and models in culture, Lévi-Strauss had described its operations as being similar to those that the algebraist does with equations [24]. "Function" here has more of a mathematical connotation, in contrast to its meaning in the label "structural-function-alism", where it refers to the contribution a part makes to the whole. Lévi-Strauss has quite rightly pointed out that Durkheim envisaged this kind of structuralist analysis of codes when he made the following statement in *The Rules of Sociological Method:*

"Myths, popular legends, religious conceptions of all sorts, moral beliefs, etc., reflect a reality different from the individual's reality; but the way in which they attract and repel each other, unite or separate, may nevertheless be independent of their content and may depend uniquely on their general quality as representations. Although their substance is different, they would behave in their mutual relations as do sensations, images, or ideas, in the individual Is it not conceivable, for example, that contiguity and resemblance, logical contrasts and antagonisms, act in the same way, whatever may be the things they represent? . . . We need to investigate, by comparison of mythical themes, popular legends, traditions, and languages, the manner in which social representations adhere to and repel one another, how they fuse or separate from one another"[25].

The structuralism of the *Annales* School and of Lévi-Strauss are both very different from the structural-functionalist sociology which came into prominence with the expansion of American sociology after the Second World War. It is ironical that Durkheim's fame should have been boosted by American sociology, which had long resisted his influence. The reviews of his works in the *American Journal of Sociology* were critical of his "social realism" and his definition of sociology's subject-matter — social facts, seen as emergent properties of a collectivity, and characterized by their exteriority and constraint in relation to the individual [26]. It went against the prevailing individualism of early American sociology and its tendency to deduce the properties of the group from the properties of its constituent individuals.

However, Durkheim had more success in influencing British sociology and anthropology during his lifttime. At the launching of the Sociological Society in 1903 the promoters enlisted his sympathy and aid. He sent them one of his programmatic statements, which they then circulated in summary form to leading sociologists throughout Europe, eliciting replies that were then discussed at length [27].

It is one of the quirks of intellectual history that the eventual successful re-entry of Durkheimian sociology into America was partly in the form of an adaptation re-exported from Britain. It was taken there by the anthropologist A. R. Radcliffe-Brown, who went to the University of Chicago for several years in the early 1930s. Radcliffe-Brown's adaptation was suited to the study of societies with little if any written history. It lost sight of Durkheim's original problematic — that of resolving the divisions and problems of a modern industrial society and of reconciling individualism and social solidarity. Radcliffe-Brown's structural-functionalism was inspired by Durkheim's studies of religion and kinship, which was not surprising in view of the fact that those were the studies in which Durkheim drew mainly on data from pre-industrial societies. When applied to American society and topics such as social stratification, as in the work of W. Lloyd Warner and Talcott Parsons, the integrating function of kinship was still given prominence. Indeed, for Parsons, who did more than anyone else to promote this structural-functionalist version of Durkheimian sociology, stratification itself was an integrating function in the social system. He placed kinship, the fundamental principle of which was solidarity, on a par with occupation in terms of relevance to stratification in an industrial society [28]. But Durkheim was quite clear in saying that the family was of declining importance in modern socity and was "becoming an agency secondary to the state" [29]. His focus included the institutional form of the state and economic association (in *Professional Ethics and Civic Morals*) and educational ideologies associated with rising social classes (in *The Evolution of Educational Thought*).

The reputation of Durkheim as a structural-functionalist has tended to obscure his other contributions. In recent years there has been an explosion of studies of Durkheim and his sociology, particularly in France. As with Marxian studies, re-appraisal has been necessitated and facilitated by the posthumous publication of some of the author's writings. This has added greatly to our knowledge of his work, and in the case of previously unpublished letters and papers it has shed new light on Durkheim's activities and opinions. However, all of this only increases the profusion of different interpretations of his sociology which derive from different ways of reading his works. Some scholars have sought to understand the work in the intellectual and social context of its own time, others read it in terms of their own personal and political concerns. Another approach has been to examine the work for its contribution to certain theories, thematic ideas, or problems regarded as currently constitutive of the discipline of sociology. This latter strategy was followed by Parsons and has been admitted to by another influential commentator, LaCapra [30]. In such a way a discipline may constitute itself, reducing the texts to fit in with some disciplinary paradigm, rather than examining them on their own terms and in their original context. We will find that these reductive readings are contested by the "founding" texts themselves in significant ways. Such readings may have rendered the texts more operational for organized research, but it has been at the cost of making them less multifaceted and less critical.

Used judiciously, both these approaches can add something to the understanding of founding works such as those of Durkheim. In order to understand what Durkheim was advocating it is necessary to be aware of what he was against, and that entails placing his thought in the context of his time and taking account of his private expressions of opinion in letters and reported conversations. In this respect we are fortunate now in having available previously unknown letters, some of which were made public for the first time in the *Revue francaise de sociologie* (1976 and 1979). It also adds to our appreciation of his achievement to trace the ways in which he influenced or anticipated later developments in sociology, without trying to squeeze his intellectual development in the direction of some present-day paradigm, which is a criticism that has been levelled against Parsons. This book will attempt to get the best out of both these strategies. Firstly, it will take account of the latest findings on the texts, their context, and information on Durkheim's life and opinions. Secondly, we will consider Durkheim's work critically in the light of subsequent developments.

However, we are aware that there can be no "innocent" reading of texts, as the French Marxist Louis Althusser made clear in his *Reading 'Capital'* (with E. Balibar)[31]. In the following chapters we will provide a generally sympathetic reading of Durkheim's texts, but it is a sympathy cultivated for the purpose of understanding his work, not for advocating total conversion to his point of view. Rather than responding to this problem about reading texts by making only general statements, as though attempting an "innocent" reading by cultivating vagueness, we will plead guilty to the following tendencies in reading Durkheim:

Politically, he does not fit easily under current labels. Some commentators take a wholly negative view of his politics and label him as a conservative apologist for the status quo and a defender of buorgeois interests [32]. Others label him as a socialist [33]. We will try to avoid labelling him, but rather examine his positions on specific issues. This will involve making judgements about the degree of commitment that he had to specific causes, doctrines, and reforms. His most important commitment was to educational reform, that at least is clear. He made statements from time to time about the need to reduce inequalities, and spoke of the need to abolish the inheritance of private property. He had a theory of politics that overlapped with socialism; he associated with and encouraged socialists; but he did not commit himself to socialism. To the extent that he was anti-Marxist, it was based on an opposition to what he took to be unscientific Marxism then current in France, which was economic determinist, and his scorn for the sectarian Marxist groups. He made important contributions to "corporative theory" and to the movement for "solidarist syndicalism" [34]. We will see that this contribution is now topical again in view of the revival of interest in theories of corporatism. (By corporatism is meant a political structure which integrates organized socio-economic producer groups, which control their own sectors of the economy in partnership with the State, as in the case of British agriculture and the National Farmers Union). Durkheim was interested in developing corporatism in a more democratic direction, and as a buffer between the individual and the State. A recent full-length study by Filloux, *Durkheim et le socialisme* (1977), concludes that "The originality of Durkheim was to situate the corporative system in the general theory of democracy and of socialism"[35].

Intellectually, he will be judged to have made the greatest contribution of any single individual to the development of sociology as a scholarly discipline. By any standard Durkheim's scholarly achievement must be judged impressive. At the age of forty he had already written three of the classic texts of sociology — *The Division of Labour in Society, The Rules of Sociological Method,* and *Suicide.* Each of these works demonstrated the sociological method for disclosing relationships between different layers of the total social phenomenon. In the *Division of Labour* it was relationships between such factors as population density (including density of interactions), specialization of functions, and the legal and penal system. In the *Rules* he discussed the method in more detail and with illustrations from the division of labour and suicide. *Suicide* itself demonstrated that the most complex structural relationships could be plotted by using an empirical indicator such as differential suicide rates. The underlying theme, as in the other works, was the way in which structural relationships affect the level of social integration. Low suicide rates revealed a "healthy" level of integration; high suicide rates revealed pathological states.

In his last great work, *The Elementary Forms of the Religious Life,* Durkheim gave his most compelling demonstration of the structuralist method, tracing relationships between social organization, religious beliefs, and such fundamental categories of thought as space, time, and causation. He seemed to have brought about the "sociologization of everything".

Despite the cosmic implications, Durkheim's sociology was, like the man himself, cool and analytical. There was none of the prophetic flavour that is to be found in Marx's writings, nor the torment of Max Weber's vision of man caught in the iron cage of bureaucratic society. Durkheim focused on a limited number of subjects and dealt with them from many angles. The fascination of his approach lies in its capacity to surprise. He penetrates to the deeper layers of structure by way of the most oblique routes. And we are surprised to discover how far we have advanced in our understanding after following him down these by-ways. Sometimes the going is dull, but then he will suddenly produce paradoxes that revive our interest. If the subject is the division of labour — a weighty topic that can become all too heavy — it is a relief to be teased with the suggestion that punishment of crime is designed to act more on the law-abiding citizen than on the criminal [36]. When feeling depressed by the subject-matter of *Suicide,* it is thought-provoking to come across the proposition that marriage is harmful to women (without children) if we are to judge from the different suicide rates [37]. In *The Elementary Forms of the Religious Life,* a painstaking account of totemism among Australian aborigines and American indians brings us face to face with the possibility that God is society, and that our basic ideas of time, space, and causation may reflect past and present social organization [38].

None of these statements is imposed on the reader as a sweeping assertion, but couched as a sociological hypothesis with a sample of empirical supporting evidence. By such means Durkheim succeeded in establishing the positive basis that Comte's sociology lacked.

REFERENCES

[1] Claude Lévi-Strauss, "French Sociology", in Goerges Gurvitch

and Wilbert E. Moore (eds.), *Twentieth Century Sociology*, New York, Philosophical Library Inc., 1945, 503-537, p. 505. Cf. on Comte's prospectus for sociology, Kenneth Thompson, *Auguste Comte: The Foundation of Sociology*, London, Thomas Nelson, 1976.

[2] Cf. Durkheim's contribution in H. Dagan, *Enquete sur l'anti-sémitisme*, Paris, P. V. Stock, 1899, pp. 59-63.

[3] Marcel Mauss, "Th. Ribot et les sociologues", in *Centennaire de Théodule Ribot, Jubile de la psychologie scientifique francaise*, Paris, Agen, 1939, 137-8, p. 138.

[4] E. Durkheim, Review of G. Richard, *Le Socialisme et la science sociale*, in *Revue philosophique*, XLIV, 1897, pp. 200-205.

[5] Durkheim, Review of L. Gumplowicz, *Grundriss der Soziologie*, in *Revue philosophique*, **20**, 1885, pp. 627-34, p. 627.

[6] Durkheim, Review of A. Schäffle, *Bau und Leben des sozialen Körpers: Erster Band, Revue philosophique*, XIX, 1885, pp. 84-101.

[7] Ibid, translation in Mark Traugott (ed.), *Emile Durkheim on Institutional Analysis*, Chicago, University of Chicago Press, 1978, p. 102.

[8] Ibid, p. 103.

[9] Durkheim, "Sociology and Its Scientific Field", in Kurt, H. Wolff (ed.), *Emile Durkheim et al, Essays on Sociology and Philosophy*, New York, Harper and Row, 1960, 355-75, p. 369. (Originally published as "La sociologia ed il suo dominio scientifico" in *Rivista Italiana di Sociologia*, IV, 1900, pp. 127-48.

[10] Ibid., p. 373.

[11] Durkheim, *The Rules of Sociological Method*, trs. by S. A. Solovay and J. H. Mueller, Chicago, University of Chicago Press, 1938, pp. XXXIX-XLIII. (Originally published as *Les Règles de la méthode sociologique*, Paris Alcan, 1895).

[12] Review of Antonio Labriola, *Essais sur la conception matérialiste de l'histoire*, in *Revue philosophique*, **44**, 1897, pp. 645-51, translation from Traugott, op. cit., p. 127.

[13] Ibid, p. 130.

[14] Thomas, M. Dando, *"L'Année sociologique:* From Durkheim to Today", *Pacific Sociological Review*, **19**, 1976, pp. 147-74.

[15] Cf. Terry N. Clark, *Prophets and Patrons: The French University and the Emergence of the Social Sciences*, Cambridge, Mass., Harvard University Press, 1973, p. 183.

[16] "Emile Durkheim" in *Sociological Review*, X, 1, 1918, p. 54; and Victor Branford, "Durkheim: A Brief Memoir", *Sociological*

Review X, 2, 1918, 77-82, p. 77.

[17] See the reviews of *L'Année sociologique* by Albion Small in *American Journal of Sociology*, V, 1899, p. 124; III, 1898, p. 700; VI, 1900, pp. 276-7; VIII, 1902, pp. 277-8; XI, 1905, pp. 132-3.
See the slightly ironical editors' footnotes accompanying a report of a discussion at the *London Sociological Society*, in *AJS*, X, 1, 1904, pp. 120-26. As an example of rivalry between the conceptions of sociology held by the *AJS* and *L'Année*, and of the status competition, see Albion Small's review of *L'Année* in *AJS*, XI, 1905, pp. 132-33.

[18] "Prefaces to L'Année Sociologique" in Wolff, op. cit., 341-53, p. 342.

[19] Ibid, p. 343.

[20] Cf. R. Colbert Rhodes, "Emile Durkheim and the Historical Thought of Marc Bloch", *Theory and Society*, 5, 1, 1978, pp. 45-73.

[21] Fernand Braudel, "Personal Testimony", *Journal of Modern History*, 44, 1, 1972, 448-67, p. 456.

[22] Robert Forster and Orest Ranum (eds.), *Rural Society in France: Sections from the Annales Economies, Sociétés, Civilisations*, Baltimore, John Hopkins University Press, 1977, p. vii.

[23] "Sociology and its Scientific Field", in Wolff, op. cit., 354-75, p. 362.

[24] Claude Lévi-Strauss, *Structural Anthropology*, 2, New York, Basic Books, 1976, p. 24.

[25] Author's Preface to Second Edition of *The Rules* . . ., op. cit., p. I.

[26] See the following reviews: G. Tosti, "The Delusions of Durkheim's Sociological Objectivism", *American Journal of Sociology*, IV, 1898, pp. 171-77; Tosti, "Suicide in the Light of Recent Studies", *AJS*, III, 1898, pp. 464-78.

[27] Durkheim (with E. Fauconnet), "Relation of Sociology to the Social Sciences and to Philosophy" in *Sociological Papers*, 1904, and reprinted in the *Sociological Review*, X, 2, 1918, pp. 77-82.

[28] Cf. Talcott Parsons, "Social Classes and Class Conflict in the Light of Recent Sociological Theory", in his *Essays in Sociological Theory*, New York, Free Press, 1964, pp. 323-35. In addition to developing the structural-functionalist version of Durkheim after the Second World War, Parsons had also provided an influential reinterpetation of Durkheim's sociology in T. Parsons, *The Structure of Social Action*, New York, McGraw-Hill, 1937.

[29] Durkheim, *Moral Education*, New York, Free Press, Paperback

edn. 1973, p. 75.

[30] Parsons, op. cit., 1937; Dominick LaCapra, "Rethinking Intellectual History and Reading Texts", in *History and Theory*, XIX, 3, 1980, pp. 245–76, and his *Emile Durkheim: Sociologist and Philosopher*, Ithaca, Cornell University Press, 1972.

[31] London, New Left Books, 1970. Two readings of Durkheim's sociology which reveal the influence of Althusser are: G. Therborn, *Science, Class and Society*, London, New Left Books, 1976, and Paul Q. Hirst, *Durkheim, Bernard and Epistemology*, London and Boston, Routledge and Kegan Paul, 1975.

[32] Cf. Irving M. Zeitlin, *Idealogy and the Development of Sociological Theory*, Englewood Cliffs, N. J., Prentice-Hall, 1968; Joseph, R. Llobera, "Durkheim, the Durkheimians and their collective misrepresentation of Marx", *Social Science Information*, 19, 2, 1980, pp. 385–411. A commentary which provides a sympathetic account of conservative elements in Durkheim's sociology is Robert A. Nisbet, *The Sociology of Emile Durkheim*, New York, Oxford University Press, 1974.

[33] Cf. Terry N. Clark, 1973, op. cit., p. 190, and Jean-Claude Filloux, *Durkheim et le socialisme*, Geneva and Paris, Librairie Droz, 1977.

[34] M. H. Elbow, *French Corporative Theory, 1789–1948*, New York, Columbia University Press, 1953; J. E. S. Hayward, "Solidarist Synicalism: Durkheim and Duguit", *Sociological Review*, 8, 1959, pp. 17–36 and 185–202.

[35] Filloux, op. cit., p. 350.

[36] *The Division of Labour in Society*, New York, Free Press paperback edn., 1964, p. 108.

[37] *Suicide*, Glencoe, Ill., Free Press, 1951, pp. 188–9.

[38] *The Elementary Forms of the Religious Life*, New York, Free Press, paperback edn., 1965, p. 257 and 21–25.

2

Life and Intellectual Background

Durkheim is often ranked alongside Marx and Weber to form a triumvirate of key figures whose influence on the development of sociology is unparalleled. To many sociologists he epitomizes the founding father figure in academic sociology. Unlike Marx or Weber he actually defined his vocation in terms of a mission to develop sociology as an accepted and esteemed discipline within the university world, and he identified closely with that professional role. It is the key to his character and to his work. With regard to his character, Marcel Mauss described him as "the professional conscience personified"[1]. Furthermore, in terms of professional priorities, he sacrificed many of his own projects (including, unfortunately, a projected book on current developments in socialist thought, which included Marxism), to the founding and editing of *l'Année sociologique*. He was convinced that the journal, by its scope and scholarship, could do more for the establishment of sociology than any single work. In the preface to the second edition of his own work, *The Rules of Sociological Method*, he was able to report that:

"It is nonetheless true that, in recent years, in spite of opposition, the cause of objective, specific, and methodological sociology has gained ground continuously. The founding of the *Année socio-logique* has certainly contributed much to this result. Because it embraces the entire field of the science, the *Année* has been able, better than any more limited enterprise, to establish a standard which sociology must, and will, achieve"[2].

It is worth emphasizing the professional orientation of Durkheim and viewing his life and work within that context not only because that accords with his own view of himself, but also because there are few intimate or revealing pieces of information available that would justify giving prominence to any other slant. The most revealing psycho-logical assessment of Durkheim by a friend, Georges Davy, simply serves to support this view of him as devoted to the academic life, which "perhaps even went to the point of preventing him from enjoying without scruples any pleasure except the Spinoza-like joy which is brought by enthusiasm for an idea"[3]. An anecdote that confirms the portrait of Durkheim as an austerely dedicated academic is to the effect that his nephew and collaborator, Mauss, when a mature scholar, once hid in fright when, sitting drinking coffee at a café opposite the Sorbonne, he saw his uncle approaching. His fear was that Durkheim would chastise him for not working.

Durkheim's devotion to the academic life and to developing sociology can be understood in terms of biographical facts without recourse to much psychological speculation. He was originally expected to follow in his father's footsteps and become a rabbi, and to this end he attended rabbinical school for a time. Why he gave up this intention and how he lost his Jewish religious belief is not known. The only religious incident during his schooldays that has been recorded concerns a brief mystical experience that he went through under the influence of a Catholic schoolmistress. From this point on his main striving was for academic success. His chosen path does not seem to have been an easy one at first. He had all the anxieties of a bright boy from a religious family of modest means and who is imbued with a high sense of responsi-bility and vocation, and an ambition to succeed. In his early years as a student in Paris he seems to have lived in fear of failure, or at least of not meeting the expectations people had of him. Despite his brilliant record at secondary school in Epinal, when sent to Paris to prepare for the examination to gain entrance to the Ecole Normale Superieur he failed two years in succession and succeeded only at the third attempt. He then became one of the outstanding students at ENS, but in his

final year he developed a serious skin disease that often has psychoso-
matic origins, and finished in next to last place in the *agrégation* (the
qualifying examination for teaching posts in French high schools) [4].

Durkheim does not appear to have been very happy at ENS even
though former fellow students' remarks indicate that he was always in
the centre of arguments and debates. The famous philospher, Henri
Bergson, who was a year ahead of Durkheim during their time there, is
the source for a critical remark that has gained widespread currency,
to the effect that Durkheim was always propounding theories, and when
told that the facts contradicted them, replied that the facts were wrong
[5]. However, Bergson's highly speculative, vitalist philosphy, was
precisely the kind of unscientific doctrine that Durkheim vehemently
opposed, and it is ironical that the charge of ignoring the facts should
come from that source. Even as students there must have been rivalry
and incompatibility of views between Bergson and Durkheim, and this
may account for the story. There were frequent debates, sometimes
arranged by the professors, who wished to test the students against
each other. One such was between Bergson and Jean Jaurès, the future
socialist leader, and close friend of Durkheim [6].

In some ways ENS was a disappointment to Durkheim, and he had
ambivalent feelings about his time there. Although he valued the
opportunities it offered for serious study, and he later sent his son André
there, during his own period in residence he resented the classical and
literary bias to the studies and the general air of snobbery of an intellectual elite. As one of his fellow students, Holleaux, later recollected:

> "I have seen him ardently wishing for the end of the year, the
> vacation time, the momemt he would be allowed to live again
> among 'good simple people' (his own expression). Being absolutely
> simple, he detested all affection. Being deeply serious, he hated a
> flippant tone"[4].

However, although Durkheim may have been disappointed in the
content of some of the teaching, he was clearly greatly concerned
with the serious political and social issues that were being debated in
ENS. Jaurès admitted that it was Durkheim who nudged him towards a
greater preoccupation with social problems [6]. This was the period of
struggle to establish the Third Republic on a democratic basis and to
undertake social reconstruction, particularly through the provision of
free, secular education. The two outstanding leaders in this struggle,
Léon Gambetta and Jules Ferry, had both been greatly influenced by
the sociology of Comte, as mediated through his follower Emil Littré,
who acted as the mentor of the younger republican generation that

came to leadership in the 1870s [7]. Gambetta spoke of Comte as the greatest thinker of the century and used him as an authority when advocating the teaching of science in the elementary schools of France. Ferry, for his part, confessed that Comte's philosophy came as a revelation to him. Durkheim seems to have identified with their position from an early stage, as did many of those with his kind of background.

Many other influences were to shape Durkheim's intellectual and political orientation, but none was more important than this initial exposure to a fusion of Comtist sociology and reformist republicanism. Its effect was to bring him to a similar view of the relation between sociology and politics as that which Littré had formed in adapting Comte's teachings. Indeed, it might be said that Durkheim modified and developed Comte's sociology as Littré had adapted the political implications of his teaching. Littré showed that Comte's attempt to guide political policies with principles drawn from sociology need not, as they did in Comte's own case, lead to authoritarianism. Durkheim, under the guidance of his teacher Émile Boutroux, at ENS, was led to a closer reading of Comte's sociology and set about purging it of some of the dogmatism that had brought it into disrepute in academic circles. From Boutroux and Comte he took the notion that the field of each science was irreducible to that of any other, and so sociology could not be reduced to a biologically-based psychology, just as biology could not be reduced to the physico-chemical sciences. Sociology had to have its own distinctive subject-matter and principles of explanation.

Another important influence on the development of Durkheim's thought during his time at ENS was the philosopher Charles Renouvier, who was also a major influence on the thinking of liberal republicans in the last decades of the nineteenth century. The ideas that attracted Durkheim were Renouvier's uncompromising rationalism, his central concern with morality and the need to study it scientifically, his modification of Kant's ideas into what he called 'criticism': an attempt to reconcile determinism in the world of matter with the concept of human freedom and morality. He taught that there existed a real, phenomenal world, bound together according to natural laws, and by necessary connections such as cause and effect. But man must be understood as a rational, self-determining being who stood outside the phenomenal sequence in respect to his moral decisions and moral freedom. Progress through mastery over nature was possible, but conditional on moral progress based on man's mastery over himself and his own actions. 'Criticism', as a method, involved an analysis of reason and of the nature of the world, which in turn required much historical research [8].

Renouvier thus combined a concern with the dignity and autonomy of the individual and a theory of social cohesion based on the individual's sense of unity with and dependence on others. Durkheim's subsequent opposition to the powerful doctrines of utilitarianism, which were dominant in contemporary economic and political theories, particularly those emanating from Britain, was derived in part from Renouvier's preference for principles of justice over those of utility, and a denial that the former could be derived from the latter. Renouvier's view that contemporary socity was in a state of war led him to advocate that the State should perform the role of establishing justice in the eoncomic sphere, and to complement this he advocated associations independent of the State, such as producers' cooperatives. Like all the liberal and radical republicans he emphasized the need for secular education in state schools. Durkheim took over Renouvier's purpose of reconciling the sacredness of the individual, and respect for individual dignity, with social solidarity.

Lukes has pointed out that there may be a more fundamental respect in which Renouvier may have influenced Durkheim [9]. Renouvier interpreted and developed Kant's view that reason, and particularly categories of thought, are given *a priori,* in such a way as to stress the role of will and choice in establishing the fundamental principles that govern our experience. Renouvier's view of knowledge and reason (his epistemology) implied that categories of thought such as space, time, substance, cause, etc., could be other than they were. Durkheim developed this into a sociological epistemology which implied that categories ordering thought and experience varied from society to society and were socially determined. This position was developed by Durkheim in his essay with Marcel Mauss, *Primitive Classification,* and in his *The Elementary Forms of the Religious Life.*

In addition to these philosophical influences, Durkheim assimilated the example of his history teachers at ENS, Gabriel Monod and Fustel de Coulanges. Their rigorous historical methods made a great impression on him, and this was reflected in his own view of the need of sociology to shake off the reputation of unsubstantiated generalization, which derived from the writings of Spencer and Comte. Monod's course surveying the institutions of ancient France was full of references to specialist works and yet still managed to summarize this scientific work in a clear account. Durkheim's own later lectures on the history of education in France had the same characteristics, as can be seen in the posthumously published book, *The Evolution of Educational Thought: Lectures on the Formation and Development of Secondary Education in France.*

For Fustel de Coulanges, the author of *The Ancient City*, history was a science, and the historian had to seek to shed all personal preconceptions when analysing historical data. This was to be echoed in Durkheim's promulgation of the rubric of sociological method to the effect that the sociologist must systematically discard all preconceptions and abstain from using concepts formed outside science and for purposes that had nothing to do with science:

"He must emancipate himself from the fallacious ideas that dominate the mind of the layman; he must throw off, once and for all, the yoke of these empirical categories, which from long continued habit have become tyrannical"[2], p. 32.

Fustel de Coulanges also drew a distinction between the history of events and the history of institutions, and Durkheim was to develop this latter into a core element of sociology, which, in one of his definitions, he called "the science of institutions, their genesis and functioning"[2], p. lvi.

In *The Ancient City* extensive attention was paid to the institution of religion, especially the role of the ancestor cult in Greece and Rome; and its emphasis on the "sacred", and on the part played by ritual in establishing social bonds, was taken up by Durkheim in his *The Elementary Forms of the Religious Life*.

By the time of his *agrégation* in 1882 he had already formed an idea of the general topic on which he wished to do research for his principal doctoral thesis (he was required to write a shorter thesis in Latin, which he devoted to Montesquieu); it was to be on the relations between individualism and socialism. Subsequently the theme became somewhat modified and eventually appeared in its finished form as *The Division of Labour in Society*, but it is significant that even in its earlier form as an analysis of theories, it was concerned with social issues. This was due to Renouvier's influence, focusing philosophy on social and moral issues, as we have mentioned, but also it was due to Durkheim's natural inclination to give philosophy a sociological cast, which was accentuated by his involvement in the political debates of the time as they spilled over into the academic world. His interest in the question of the relationship of individualism and socialism arose out of his discusseion with Jaurès and other friends at ENS. As a result he was led to study the writings of Comte's mentor (and sometime employer) Henri Saint-Simon, one of the first socialist thinkers, whose work had an effect on the development of Marx's ideas [10]. Later, Durkheim was to say that Saint-Simon had not received sufficient credit from Comte and his followers for the extent to which his ideas had influenced Comte, and so sown the seed for the growth of sociology. Durkheim drew on Saint-Simon's ideas in developing his own thinking about the economic institutions in industrial society and the need for new forms of social and political organization that would take account of their centrality. It has been suggested that in going back to Saint-Simon's formulations, Durkheim was attempting a synthesis of the rival Marxist and Comtean views, combining the Comtean focus on regulating moral norms with the Marxian focus on economic institutions [11]. Durkheim's eventual proposal for occupational corporations that would provide moral regulation and own the capital confiscated in the abolition of inheritance of wealth amounted to a combination of Comtean moral rejuvenation and economic reconstruction compatible with socialist principles [12].

Durkheim made it quite clear that he regarded Saint-Simon as the inspirer of both sociology and socialism, although he gave Comte credit for having separated science from practice and so avoided Saint-Simon's tendency of rushing into hasty applications of the science before it was sufficiently established. Durkheim expressed regret that Comte and his followers, except Littré, had not given Saint-Simon sufficient credit. He was the first to free himself of the prejuices that had prevented men from submitting themselves to scientific study and to have outlined a positiveist (i.e. scientific) philosphy and sociology that would enable them to do this. In paying tribute to this achievement by Saint-Simon, Durkheim powerfully expressed his own aspiration for, and vision of, the vocation of sociology:

"To add a science to the list of sciences is always a very laborious operation, but more productive than the annexation of a new continent to old continents. And it is at once much more fruitful when the science has man for its object. It almost had to do violence to the human spirit and to triumph over the keenest resistance to make it understood that in order to act upon things it was first necessary to put them on trial. The resistance has been particularly stubborn when the material to be examined was ourselves, due to our tendency to place ourselves outside of things, to demand a place apart in the universe"[10], pp. 142–3.

It is not clear how knowledgable Durkheim was about sociology when he left ENS. He had read some of Comte's work and was sympathetic to the idea of "positivism" in the sense of studying social phenomena in the same scientific and objective manner as that used in the study of nature, and also in the sense of being opposed to the "negativism" of Englightenment philosophy to the extent that it engaged in the criticisms of institutions without promoting positive social reconstruction. But his real education in sociology seems to have taken place in the first few years after leaving ENS and whilst he was teaching at lycées in the area around Paris. By 1884 his ideas had progressed as far as the first plan of what was to become *The Division of Labour in Society*. The topic finally became defined as "the relations of the individual personality to social solidarity", and by the time of its first draft in 1886 he had come to see that "the solution to the problem belonged to a new science: sociology"[10]. In this period he set himself the task of establishing that science, of "giving it a method and a body"[10]. What had begun as a study of the relationship between individualism and socialism now became part of a project to establish a new science, sociology, and "the study of socialism was consequently interrupted"[10]. He did not go back to the study of socialism until he was teaching at the University of Bourdeaux, in 1895, and then he was so much the professional sociologist that he treated socialism simply in terms of giving a sociological explanation of socialist ideology, analyzing the social pressures that brought about its emergence [10], p. 33.

His first publication appeared whilst he was still a lycée teacher, in 1885, and it was a review of Schäffle's *Bau und Leben des sozialen Körpers*. The significance of this review, which Durkheim chose to do even though the book had been in print for some years, lies in the fact that it obviously provided him with an opportunity to set forth his own newly-developed conception of sociology. In Schäffle's work he had found his major concerns crystallized into a sociological analysis of contemporary society and a persuasive vindication of sociology itself. In many respects he was able to adopt Schäffle's views as his own. The "theoretical scaffolding", as he called it, was provided by the analogy between the biological and the social organism. This "organicist" framework implied the unity or solidarity of the collectivity over the individual part or member. This was a convenient shift in view for late nineteenth century thought from the eighteenth and early nineteenth century view which was couched in more universalistic terms. Where the earlier view saw social questions in terms of the individual in relation to "mankind" or "humanity", the organicist approach took the nation state as the societal whole on which it focused. The organicist framework was particularly relevant for French social thinkers after 1871 because it enabled them to contrast the political and ideological disunity of France with the theoretical solidarity of the French nation as an organic whole. It was a useful framework in another sense, and that was for Durkheim's purpose of getting acceptance of the need to study society scientifically. The organicist analogy served the function of implying that society was part of nature and should be studied by methods equivalent to those of the natural sciences. Although Durkheim made extensive use of the analogy in his early work, especially *The Division of Labour,* even in his review of Schäffle he was conscious of the limited usefulness of this "scaffolding" and asked: "Is it not time to tear them down in order to face things as they really are." In his later work he sought to do just that, phrasing his explanations in terms of causal factors or functional relationships, stripped of the earlier constant references to relationships between organs of the body as though that analogy was enough to explain the functioning of social phenomena. In his review of Schäffle, Durkheim maintained that sociology could not be reduced to biology because societies are united by ideal rather than material bonds, and the source of ideological unity is the collective conscience.

Durkheim's reviews brought him to the attention of the authorities, and Louis Liard, the Director of Higher Education, offered him a government scholarship to visit German universities in the academic year 1885-6.

Durkheim was greatly impressed with what he found in Germany, but his subsequent articles about it further established his reputation in the eyes of the educational authorities in France and led to his appointment to a teaching position at the University of Bordeaux in 1887. What so impressed him about the work of scholars such as Alfred Wagner, Gustav Schmoller, von Jhering, Schäffle, and Wundt, was that they had developed a social scientific approach to the study of ethics and, by relating morals to economics, the law, and other institutions, had demonstrated the social grounding and interconnectedness of these phenomena. In effect they had reasserted the *social* character of phenomena such as economics and ethics, and this was an important counterblast against the prevailing individualistic and utilitarian approach of economics and the sociology of Herbert Spencer, which were such a powerful ideological force. The so-called "economists of the chair" in Germany, including Wagner and Schmoller, reacted against the orthodox liberal economics of the time, which deduced laws from an abstract model of the market-place, in which the individual made rational economic choices, and where the state should not interfere and ethical considerations were irrelevant. Against this they put forward social theories that were inductive, social-ethical, and interventionist. The development of sociology at the end of the nineteenth century was very much affected by this reaction against the old political economy, which now seemed inadequate to deal with the rise of big corporations, class conflict, national rivalries, and the need for national unity and reconstruction.

Like Marx, Durkheim charged that the orthodox liberal economic theories that had been in the ascendant until the 1870s were ideological rather than scientific. They were ideological in that they took their basic concepts from the popular prejudices of the time, rather than developing them scientifically. Also, explanation of social events should be sought, not in terms of individuals' motives and intentions, but in terms of social structural causes that often escaped consciousness. As Durkheim put it in reviewing a Marxist work:

"We believe it is a fertile idea that social life should be explained not by the conceptions of those who participate in it, but by profound causes which escape consciousness; and we also think that these causes must principally be sought in the way in which associated individuals are grouped"[13].

At the time of his visit to Germany Durkheim can be seen to have already begun to formulate this social structuralist method of analysis. It can be seen in his exposition of Wilhelm Wundt's *Ethik,* which comprises nearly half of his article on moral science in Germany [14]. Durkheim maintained that Wundt broke with the rationalist approach to ethics by showing that reason is insufficient to explain moral ideas because they were not formed rationally. According to Wundt's "Law of the heterogenity of ends" any action produces a trail of unintended and unforeseen consequences which actually determine the moral value of the action. Thus there is a discontinuity between (rational) motives and (unpredictable) results; as a result of this the analysis of rational intentions is likely to be misleading and irrelevant when studying morality. It is necessary to focus on the results — the actual functioning — of morality in society. Similarly, Wundt's approach made clear that social explanation of moral phenomena had to treat them as facts of social existence, *sui generis.* It had to avoid the errors of methodological individualism; social customs and mores were irreducible in their origin and operation to individual acts. The goal of developing a sociology of morals was one that stayed with Durkheim throughout his life, and he was working on a book on that subject in the last year before his death.

The articles that Durkheim wrote on the basis of his trip to Germany commended him to the authorities in France as a teacher who would help to build up a secular and scientific philosophy of society, which was what seemed to be required in order to strengthen and unify France under the Third Republic. His appointment to the University of Bordeaux was to replace another republican patriot, Alfred Espinas, who had received promotion as a result of his success in developing this scientific approach in his course on pedagogy or education. Durkheim had praised Espinas' *Les Sociétés animales* (1877) as being the first attempt to study social facts in order to construct a science of them rather than to preserve the symmetry of some great philosophical system. Espinas followed Spencer, however, in his general evolutionary view of social and human development, and pictured the animal kingdom, from unicellular animals to human societies, as one continuum of life obeying a single set of natural laws. In Spencer's terms, there was an organic continuity at all levels of evolution. However, Espinas also combined with this Spencerian view the Comtean emphasis on human society as a psychic or moral entity. He did this by stating that the psychic element enters the evolutionary scale at the point where the function of reproduction necessitates a social act. Reproductive societies then evolve until they reach the large-scale level of the "herd", at which point the psychological bond, the collective consciousness, becomes one of sympathy — like-mindedness. The exchange of images (*representations*) produces an accumulation of knowledge which constitutes the intelligence of the society, and this collective consciousness takes precedence over any individual consciousness. Espinas's emphasis on the superioirity of the collective consciousness over the inidividual, and his description of the mechanism by which like-mindedness was produced in simpler societies, was drawn on by Durkheim in his own description of the mechanical solidarity based on like-mindedness in simpler societies. Espinas's attribution of superiority to the social over the individual also had political implications that are likely to have influenced Durkheim. Altruism and sympathy were to predominate over egosim, and they found their ultimate point of focus in the national society. Furthermore, this superiority of the social meant that society in the future would be organized on socialist lines, although Espinas was careful to point out that it would be a scientific socialism and not a utopian type.

The fact that Espinas's theories were based on a combination of ideas drawn from Comte and Spencer is indicative of the balance of intellectual forces at this juncture in the development of sociology in France. Both Comte and Spencer employed an evolutionary framework in their grandiose theories of human social development. The difference in emphasis was that Comte gave more importance to the stages of intellectual development in human history, tracing a development from societies where theological explanations predominated, then metaphysical thought (explanation by reference to essences), and finally the emergence of societies in which positive or scientific thought was dominant. At each stage there was a corresponding type of moral unity. Spencer placed social evolution more definitely in a process of general natural evolution. Man and society were seen as part of a cosmic process of progressive evolution, involving differentiation and specialization of the functions of parts, and a higher level of integration. In concrete social terms this involved increased division of labour and the development of harmonious mutual dependence through free exchange between individuals.

Durkheim, like Espinas, took over many of the elements of the evolutionary framework, but he did so in a critical fashion. He was particularly critical of many of Spencer's assumptions, which coincided with those of liberal economics. In mounting his critique of Spencer he adopted many of the ideas of contemporary German thinkers, because Spencer's sociology was really liberal economics writ large, or at least placed in an evolutionary framework. Ironically, Durkheim was to be accused of having developed French sociology too much along German lines as a result of taking over their emphasis on social realism in order to combat the individualist premises of the economics and Spencerian sociology stemming from England. The criticisms were put most forcefully in a book by a Catholic priest, Simon Deploige, *Le Conflict de la morale et de la sociologie* (1911) [15]. It is worth mentioning, not because Deploige's criticisms of Durkheim are very cogent, but because it does draw attention to the importance of the national factor in the development of Durkheim's sociology. The nation can be seen to have acted as the main reference for the social realism which Durkheim used to critique doctrines which reduced explanations of social phenomena to the level of individual psychology or which inflated society to the level of all humanity. Durkheim's sociological model seemed more realistic because it dealt with the confluence of social forces within a bounded society, even though he never satisfactorily defined those boundaries in sociological terms (sometimes referring to a social *species* in order to conceptualize the distinctiveness of a national identity, such as the French).

Deploige's account of the German influences on Durkheim's sociology is of interest becaust it reminds us of the relevance of the national factor when we attempt to provide a sociological analysis of the development of sociology. The factor of national rivalries, espcially intellectual reactions to wars and national defeats at the hands of a rival power, is an example of how social being determines consciousness (to use an insight common to both Marx and Durkheim). It is an example often neglected in more economistic accounts of the social determinants of sociological perspectives, which emphasize economic and class factors. Deploige suggested that Durkheim borrowed his notion of social realism from the Germans, and that its attractiveness was due to the reaction of the French to their defeat in the Franco-Prussian war of 1870. Deploige added that the German emphasis on social realism (a reality preeminently located in the nation) was in turn a reaction to Germany's defeat at the hands of Napoleon in the Battle of Jena in 1806. Although Durkheim may have got his social realism from Schäffle and Wundt, who emphasized the predominance of society as a real totality over the individuals and institutions that composed it, Deploige maintained that behind these immediate influences there were earlier German originators of this trend. He mentioned Adam Muller, who gave a series of lectures in 1808, proclaiming the nation to be a living whole. This led Deploige to proclaim him the first sociologist, according to Durkheim's conception of sociology as social realism, and in this way he hoped to smear Durkheim's sociology as a German product, and thus leave the field free for his own Catholic doctrines.

Despite Deploige's smear tactics, he did make one criticism that hit at a weak link in Durkheim's attempt to combine the German emphasis on a society as an organic whole and the evolutionary framework of Spencer. Durkheim never arrived at a definition of *society* that was conceptually consistent with his social realism and with the organic and evolutionary theoretical frameworks that he borrowed from. He appreciated that these frameworks were simply analogies, "scaffolding", that had to be transcended, but to do so would have required him to produce a new theoretical paradigm that would have yielded a theoretical object for his sociology. In his later works he was feeling his way towards a more consistently defined theoretical object, in the form of structures of consciousness with varying degrees of institutionalized embodiment. But at other times his commitment to social realism meant that the term "society" simply referred to the nation (e.g. France), or entities within it, such as the State or the family. Deploige charged that Durkheim failed to appriciate the true context and reference of social realism, because he wrenched it out of its German intellectual context in which it referred specifically to the nation, and as a result his notion of society as a "thing" became vague and mystifying:

"When Muller, Savigny, List, Roscher, Knies, Schmoller, and Wagner repeat that society is something different from the sum of its members they know what they are saying, and among themselves they are understood. They mean the *Volk,* that slow product of history, as they call it; they are thinking of the nation, that community which survives individuals, reuniting the generations by an identity of language, cult, law, morality insitutions, interests, memories, and hopes; and they rightly vindicate the title of 'realist' for the scientific tendency which they represent. Durkheim took over their formula, but no-one knows what there is within and behind it when he says that society is a being *sui generis,* because nowhere has he defined what he means by society, and as we have proved, his attempts to define the 'social fact' terminated in failure. He does not place you in the presence of a tangible object, face to face with a 'thing'. He shakes before your eyes a vague concept, a fleeting abstraction, and the Germans' postulate becomes in his writings a cabalistic formula. His social realism is like one of the sterilized plants which it has become the fashion to place in apartments without light or air"[15], pp. 174-5.

In his response to Deploige, Durkheim sought to play down the German influence on his sociology, and in doing so he not only reasserted the importance of Comte and Renouvier, but also pointed to the predominant position given to religious phenomena in his thought under the influence of British and American scholars, especially the Scotsman William Robertson Smith [16]. Despite some suggestions to the contrary, there is no break in the development of Durkheim's thought, such that it could justifiably be described as being converted from a materialist to a "spiritualist" or idealist position. Throughout his life he remained alive to the interaction between social structure and consciousness. However, there is no doubt that he did give increased attention to religious phenomena from the time that he read deeply in historical literature on religion in order to give a lecture course on that subject in 1894-5, and then in later years he absorbed a great deal of the ethnographic literature on religion in primitive societies, such as the totemic religion of Australian aboriginal clans. Robertson Smith's theory of the clan cult of totemism as the earliest and most elementary form of religion, invariably linked to societies with the simplest form of social structure, the clan segmentary system, was in line with Durkheim's own views about the all-pervasive nature of religion in simpler societies, as presented in *The Division of Labour in Society*. It was also developed as a major theme in *The Elementary Forms of the Religious Life*. In his earlier references to religion, its importance as a social phenomenon embedded in social practices, not just in the form of beliefs, was discussed mainly in terms of its function of producing social solidarity and as a source of moral unity. As such, it seemed destined to decrease in significance as societies became more complex and as its function of maintaining social solidarity was taken over by other institutions. That was the thesis of *The Division of Labour in Society*. However, as Durkheim did more research on the subject, from the time of the 1894-5 lecture course, he became more convinced that religion provided the clue to understanding the relationship between social structures and consciousness in general, and it also provided a test case for developing sociological methods of analysing symbolization in society. He maintained that symbolism made social life possible and enabled society to reproduce itself over time.

The course on religion was only one of the courses he taught at Bordeaux. His appointment was in social science and education, and so he had to teach courses on moral and intellectual education, and the history of pedagogy. Both at Bordeaux and later at the Sorbonne in Paris the opportunity to teach sociology was only given on the basis that he would devote a substantial proportion of his time to teaching education courses. There was still formidable opposition to sociology in the universities and it virtually had to be smuggled in by the back door. When he moved to the Sorbonne in 1902 it was to a post in education, rather than sociology, and he was rather reluctant to let his name go forward. It was not unitl 1913 that his Chair was made one in "Education and Sociology". Nevertheless, this had some advantages as it guaranteed that his influence would be spread widely throughout the schools of France. His course in Paris on the history and theory of education in France was compulsory for all students undertaking the *agrégation* in arts and sciences, and some critics of his influence in the education system spoke of it as "State Durkheimianism".

The fifteen years Durkheim spent at Bordeaux were perhaps the most productive of his life so far as variety of subjects taught and books written was concerned. In addition to the education courses he also lectured on the family, suicide, legal and political sociology, social solidarity, psychology, criminology, religion, the history of socialism, and the history of sociological theories. His publications included the two theses, *The Division of Labour* and the study of Montesquieu; *The Rules of Sociological Method; Suicide;* and articles on incest, the individual and collective representations, on the definition of religious phenomena, on the "Two Laws of Penal Evolution", and on totemism. By 1902 he had already founded and edited five volumes of *L'Année sociologique*, [9], p. 100.

From the time of his first public lecture at Bordeaux, when he staked out the claims for sociology, Durkheim devoted himself to building up the discipline. Rather than developing a grand theory, he presented sociology as a perspective and a method of anlaysis that could be applied in a wide range of disciplines, such as law, history and philosophy. Not surprisingly, this excited some opposition and resistance from people in other disciplines who resented what they saw as sociological imperialism. However, it also attracted disciples and adherents who were eager to follow his lead and apply his sociological perspective and method of analysis in their own specialisms. The *Année sociologique* was divided into topic sections in order to further this aim, and so gained an extensive readership among rising scholars in different fields. An indication of the scope of its coverage can be given by listing the main sections, to all of which Durkheim contributed reviews: General Sociology (including methodological issues, social theories, social psychology, and sociological conditions of knowledge), Sociology of Religion, Juridic and Moral Sociology (including sexual morality, marriage and the family, social organization, political organization, international and moral law, penal law, property law, contract and obligation), Sociology of Crime and Statistics on Morals, Economic Sociology, Social Morphology (mainly social geography), and Miscellaneous (including Aesthetic Sociology and Education) [17]. The team of scholars that Durkheim recruited were drawn mainly from ENS, the University of Bordeaux, and the Sorbonne, and they were also united in their allegiance to Durkheim and were inspired by his sociological example. The extent of this influence can be judged by the impact that it had on scholars in various disciplines and areas of study, such as historians, and specialists in ancient civilizations, the history of law, mythology, linguistics, and religion.

It is difficult to recapture the intellectual excitement and sense of mission that existed in the team of *L'Année sociologique* and the Durkheimian School of the turn of the century. Too often Durkheimian sociology is equated with its later adaptations in the form of structural-functionalism in post-Second World War American sociology, or else it is regarded as a distant historical phenomenon that has little present relevance. In fact a proper appreciation of the context and content of Durkheimian sociology will show that it has great relevance to current developments. Although another world war has taken place since Durkheim's death, and there have been many changes in intellectual fashions and in sociological currents, there are many tangible links that witness to the essential continuity between Durkheim's sociology and that of the present. There is even a thriving *Group d'études durkheimiennes* at the *Maison des Sciences de l'Homme* in Paris, with its own regularly published bulletin.

It was a recent Director of the *Maison,* the historian Fernand Braudel, who testified to the effect that Durkheim and *L'Année sociologique* had in inspiring the founders of the *Annales* School of French history, and he told of how the *Année* became the favourite reading matter for an entire generation of young historians "from Lucien Febvre to Marc Bloch, André Piganiol, and Louis Gernet". In fact, the streams of influence went in both directions — from sociology to history and back again. The overlap between the Durkheimian sociologists and the *Annales* historians was significant. Although Febvre worried about the historians being taken over completely by sociology, several historians happily wrote for both journals. In some cases, as for example, Louis Gernet, the primary loyalty did seem to be to Durkheimian sociology. The network of influences is well illustrated by Gernet, who was born in 1882 and died in 1962. He began as a classical scholar and then, under the influence of the Durkheimians, developed his interest in linguistics in a sociological direction. (The Durkheimian School in general was keenly interested in language because of its central importance as a social phenomenon, and because "positive" research in the social sciences had achieved its greatest successes in linguistics.) Gernet applied this Durkheimian sociology to the study of ancient Greece, just as another Durkheimian, Marcel Granet, was applying it to ancient China. Gernet wrote for the *Annales* and for the *Année* (in the last decade of his life he was general secretary and chief editor of the *Année*).

From 1905 Gernet was also a member of the socialist study group formed under the influence of Lucien Herr, the Librarian of the Ecole Normale, as were many of the Durkheimians, such as Mauss, Simiand, Halbwachs, Granet, Hertz, Levi-Bruhl, and others. He contributed to the group's periodical, *Notes critiques: sciences sociales,* as did Durkheim himself in the form of reviews. This fact illustrates the overlap between these various networks and gives an indication of the general ideological atmosphere and intellecutal milieu in which they carried on their collaboration. It should be remembered that even at Bordeaux Durkheim's students organized a socialist study circle, which studied Marx's *Capital.* They also joined with the Workers' Party at Bordeaux in inviting the socialist leader, Jaurès, to speak. Jaurès took the opportunity of extolling Durkheim's work. And when Durkheim gave his course on the history of socialist ideas, Jaurès and the other socialist leader Guesde expressed agreement with his definition of socialism. He intended to give a further course on Marx and German socialism, but instead he found that editing *L'Année sociologique* left him no time. According to Mauss, Durkheim always regretted his inability to continue or resume his history of socialism.

In a sense, Durkheim's founding of *L'Année sociologique* amounted to a decision to devote himself to promoting the academic discipline of sociology rather than the political cause of socialism, even though he "sympathized" with socialism. As Mauss put it, "in 1896 Durkheim, undertaking *L'Année sociologique,* returned to pure science". Two standard reasons that are given to explain this are: firstly, he had always maintained that sociology would only be established as a science if it resisted the temptation to rush into hasty social prognostications; secondly, he disliked certain features of the socialist movement, such as its violent nature and class character, and in practice, he could not bear to submit himself to a party or political discipline.

However, Durkheim could get involved in political events, as was shown by his firm stand during the Dreyfus Affair, when he was active in the organization set up to defend human rights and to demand justice for the wrongly-condemned Captain Dreyfus, who was the victim of an upsurge of antisemitism in France. Durkheim defined the issue as one of morality and not simply politics. The article that he wrote on the subject, "Individualism and the Intellectuals" (1898) was characteristically analytical, although there was no doubt about the passionate commitment of Durkheim and the Durkheimians to the cause. They had been attacked by a conservative anti-Dreyfusard, Brunetière, who charged that the intellectuals supporting Drefus were undermining traditional institutions and spreading individualism and anarchy. In response, Durkheim drew a distinction between the individualism of utilitarianism and liberal economics, which he described as egosim, and individualism as a set of ideals in which the human person was a sacred object. He maintained that modern society needed such a "religion" or collective conscience (in contrast with his earlier position in *The Division of Labour,* where he appeared to forecast a declining role for the collective conscience). Society needed a set of collective beliefs and practices that had a special authority, and in modern society this was the "cult of the individual". He traced the social causes that had led to the emergence of this ideology, and pointed out that it was possible to be an individualist while still asserting that the individual is a product of society rather than its cause. He then added his own statement of political allegiance to this modern form of individualism, which he believed had passed through liberalism and was now pointing towards socialism:

"Our fathers undertook exclusively the task of freeing the individual from the political shackles which impeded his development. . . . We must go beyond the results achieved, if only to preserve them. If we do not finally learn to put to work the means of action we have in our hands, they will indubitably lose their worth. Let us therefore make use of our liberties to seek out what we must do and to do it, to smooth the functioning of the social machine, still so harsh on individuals, to place within their reach all possible means of developing their abilities without hindrance, to work finally to make a reality of the famous precept: to each according to his labour!"[18].

At the end of the article Durkheim distinguished between three groups of supporters of a political cause — "apostles who let their anger or their enthusiasm overflow", "scholars who bring us the product of their research and reflections", and "men of letters seduced by an interesting theme". The latter group, who played "dilettantes' games", he despised. He chose for himself the second course, and insisted that the professor should not use the authority of his position to exercise political influence over his students. At times he seemed to fear that his collaborators in the enterprise of building up sociology through *L'Année sociologique* would be swept away and become mainly apostles of socialism. After the Dreyfus Affair period, when the Durkheimian sociologists and the socialist group were almost fused into one, Durkheim became even more convinced that his vocation was to build up sociology as a scholarly discipline and that this could not be combined with political involvement. His ideas continued to exercise an influence in politics, however, through his collaborators and students. His concept of "social solidarity" exercised an influence on the amorphous movement known as "Solidarism", which became virtually the official ideology of the Third Republic in the two decades before the First World War. But his ideas about the need for a fundamental moral regeneration of society, based on greater social justice and equality, went much further towards socialism than the rather timid proposals for legislative reforms put forward by solidarists.

The fact that Durkheim devoted so much of his life to the sociological analysis of religion, should not be construed as a sign that he had decided other social phenomena such as politics and economics were unimportant.[†] Rather, he took religion as an example of ideology that

_____

[†] Attempts have been made to give a psycho-analytical explanation of Durkheim's avoidance of political action and of his alleged turning from an early political problematic to a later religious problematic. Bernard Lacroix suggests that Durkheim's reticence in the face of political action may have been due to a castration anxiety, and that his wish to change the world at a distance, through his writings, came from a desire for identification with his father. Lacroix's most important point is that the substitution of a religious problematic for a political problematic can be interpreted by a reappearance of religious repression following the death of Durkheim's father. Cf. Lacroix, *Durkheim et le politique*, Paris, Presses de la Fondation Nationale des Sciences Politiques, 1981. For criticisms of this thesis, see Philippe Besnard, "Une etude sur Durkheim et le politique" in *Études durkheimiennes: Bulletin d'information*, 6, Juin 1981, pp. 1-5.

could be sociologically analysed to reveal its relation to social structures, which caused it to develop, and which it functioned to maintain and reproduce. He made it clear that the same kind of sociological analysis could be applied to political and economic ideologies. Among his last publications before his death were a wartime pamphlet criticizing German nationalist ideology and, testifying to his other concerns, an article for the International Exhibition at San Francisco, stating his view of sociology, and an obituary for his son, who had been a linguist and one of the most promising of the new generation of sociologists in the *Année* group [19].

REFERENCES

[1] Marcel Mauss, "In Memoriam: L'Oeuvre inédite de Durkheim et de ses collaborateurs", *Année sociologique,* new series 1, 1923, p. 9.

[2] E. Durkheim, *The Rules of Sociological Method,* trs. by S. A. Solovay and J. H. Mueller, Chicago, University of Chicago Press, 1938, p. xlii.

[3] Georges Davy, "Emile Durkheim", *Revue francaise de sociologie,* 1, 1960, 3-24, p. 6.

[4] G. Davy, "Emile Durkheim: L'Homme", *Revue de métaphysique et de morale,* xxvi, 1919, 181-98, p. 187.

[5] J. Chevalier, *Entretiens avec Bergson,* Paris, 1959, p. 34.

[6] Harvey Goldberg, *The Life of Jean Jaurès,* Madison, Univeristy of Wisconsin Press, 1962, p. 16.

[7] Cf. John Eros, "The Positivist Generation of French Republicanism", *Sociological Review,* N.S. 3, 2, 1955, 255-77.

[8] John S. Scott, *Republican Ideas and the Liberal Tradition in France, 1870-1914,* New York, Columbia University Press, 1951, pp. 56-7.

[9] Steven Lukes, *Emile Durkheim: His Life and Work,* London, Penguin, 1975, p. 56.

[10] Marcel Mauss, Introduction to the first edition, Emile Durkheim, *Socialism,* edited and with an introduction by Alvin W. Gouldner, translated by Charlotte Sattler, New York, Collier Books, 1962, p. 32.

[11] Alvin Gouldner's introduction to Durkheim's *Socialism,* [10], p. 20.

[12] cf. the proposals in Durkheim, *Professional Ethics and Civic Morals.,* trans. by C. Brookfield, London, Routledge and Kegan Paul, 1957, pp. 216-18.

[13] Durkheim, Review of Antonio Labriola, *Essais sur la conception materialiste de l'histoire,* originally published in 1897, reprinted in Mark Traugott (editor and translator), *Emile Durkheim on Institutional Analysis,* London and Chicago, University of Chicago Press, 1978, 123–30, p. 127.

[14] Durkheim, "La Science positive de la morale en Allemagne", *Revue philosophique,* xxiv (1887), 33–58, 113–42, 275–84.

[15] Simon Deploige, *Le Conflit de la morale et de la sociologie,* Louvain, Institut Superieur de Philosophie, 1911; published in English as *The Conflict Between Ethics and Sociology,* trans. C. C. Miltner, London and St Louis, Herder, 1938.

[16] Durkheim's review of Deploige's book appeared in *L'Année sociologique,* **12,** 1913, pp. 326–28.

[17] English translations of Durkheim's contribution to most of these sections are available in Yash Nandan (ed.), *Emile Durkheim: Contributions to L'Année Sociologique,* New York, Free Press and London, Collier Macmillan, 1980.

[18] "Individualism and the Intellectuals", in Robert N. Bellah (ed.), *Emile Durkheim on Morality and Society,* Chicago, University of Chicago Press, 1973, 43–57, pp. 55–56.

[19] *L'Allemagne au-dessus de tout: la mentalité allemande et la guerre,* Paris, Colin, 1915; "La Sociologie" in *La Science francaise,* Paris, Ministère de l'Instruction Publiq et des Beaux-Arts, vol. 1, pp. 39–49; "Notice sur André-Armand Durkheim", *L'Annuaire de le l'Association des anciens élèves de l'École Normale Supérieur,* pp. 201–5.

3

The Work

3.1 INTRODUCTION

There are various ways of approaching Durkheim's work, and no single approach is entirely satisfactory. In this section it is proposed to adopt a combination of approaches in order to achieve maximum flexibility and coverage, whilst avoiding the temptation to squeeze Durkheim's varied and uneven contributions into a single tidy framework. One approach that will be used as an organizing device is the "bio-bibliographical" approach. This entails taking some of the most famous of Durkheim's works in chronological order: *The Division of Labour in Society* (1893), *The Rules of Sociological Method* (1895), *Suicide* (1897), and *The Elementary Forms of the Religious Life* (1912). The advantage of this approach is that it proceeds by way of the peaks of Durkheim's range of scholarly publications, and it can also be related to a biographical sequence of events. In this way we proceed from an examination of a doctoral thesis, *The Division of Labour*, in which Durkheim set out the main themes of his life's work. We then move to the aggressively challenging methodological treatise, *The Rules*, where the author throws down the gauntlet as champion of a new and rigorous social science. In *Suicide* the ambitious young Bordeaux professor provides a substantive demonstration of the new method at work. Finally we come to the mature work, *The Elementary Forms,* which represents the culumination of Durkheim's theoretical development and the distillation of his specialized studies of religion in relation to the moral and cognitive bases of social solidarity.

The disadvantages of this conventional approach are that it tends to neglect Durkheim's other important works, some of which were published posthumously on the basis of lecture notes, and it gives an over-simplified view of his intellectual development. A second approach, which seeks to avoid these faults, treats Durkheim's work in terms of certain key concepts, unit ideas, or perspectives [1]. Robert Nisbet discerned five such perspectives in Durkheim's thought focusing on society, authority, the religio-sacred, personality and development. This approach has the virtue of providing a basis for comparing Durkheim's sociology with that of other writers, before and after him, who operated with similar ideas and perspectives. However, the selection of the particular ideas to focus on derives from a prior judgement about the important trends in this area of intellectual history. It is clear that Nisbet, and others who use this approach, wish to use Durkheim to buttress a thesis about the development of sociology or social thought, rather than taking as their primary objective the task of doing full justice to the unique character of Durkheim's own work. This selective approach is particularly misleading when a certain concept or perspective is singled out for emphasis because it fits in with the commentator's own theoretical or research interests. An example of this is the concept of "function" and the functionalist perspective, which figured prominently in the works of two of the most famous of Durkheim's interpreters, A. R. Radcliffe-Brown, the British social anthropologist, and Talcott Parsons.

Certainly Durkheim made many references to function, beginning with *The Division of Labour* where he stated that one of his objectives was to determine "the function of division of labour, that is to say, what social need it satisfies", and concluding in *The Elementary Forms of the Religious Life* with a demonstration of the integrative function performed in society by religion and each of its components - cult, rite, and symbol. In *The Rules* he stated that the task of the social researcher entailed distinguishing the efficient causes of any social pheonomenon and tracing its history, and should then lead on to an attempt to determine the function of the phenomenon in the system or order of which it was a part. However, Durkheim's emphasis on historical investigation alongside functionalist analysis was subsequently neglected in so-called functionalist sociology and anthropology.

The following discussion begins with an outline of the main components of Durkheim's sociology, including key concepts and ideas, and then proceeds to an account of his most famous works. This is then followed by a discussion of his contribution to the analysis of various social institutions, such as education, politics and the State, which will allow us to draw on other books — for example, *The Evolution of Educational Thought, Professional Ethics and Civic Morals,* and *Socialism.*

3.2 SOCIOLOGY – ITS NATURE AND PROGRAMME

3.2.1 General orientation

Durkheim can be considered as one of the first professional, university-based, sociologists, and that became his self-definition and chosen vocation. However, he began his career as a philosopher, and throughout his working life he spend much of his time lecturing on the theory and practice of pedagogy. Furthermore, he always hoped to lay the foundations for a science of morals. In these and other respects he was led beyond the confines of a single academic discipline, and he can be seen as bridging two intellectual eras — the pre-twentieth century era of wide-ranging social philosophies, and the present era of narrower, academic specialization.

One of the characteristics of an academic disipline such as sociology is that scientific progress proceeds by way of developing increasingly refined and specific definitions and hypotheses. Durkheim played a preeminent part in promoting that development in the newly-emerging discipline of sociology. But because they emerged from a much broader and looser tradition of social philosophical debate, Durkheim's sociological concepts bear many traces of the earlier polemics and polarizations. In order to understand and evaluate his concepts it is necessary to take into account these background features that provided many of the "givens" that enter into their formulation. It is also worth noting that Durkheim's thought did not always confine itself within the restricting bounds set by definitions. Sometimes he operated with more than one definition of a concept, and his ideas frequently raced ahead of the ground staked out by the definitions. Indeed, the basic concept of *society* seemed to intoxicate him[†] and escaped definition.

---

† Morris Ginsberg observed, "in general 'la societé' had an intoxicating effect on his mind"[2].

Although society and the social entered into many of his definitions of specific phenomena, society as a composite whole never received an adequate definition and could refer to phenomena as disparate as France or a married couple. Durkheim's main concern was to impress on his readers the potency of society and the social, in reaction against prevailing philosophies that were fundamentally individualist in emphasis.

Because the dichotomy of society and individual is so fundamental to Durkheim's thinking it is worth examining it in some detail. What Durkheim opposed was "methodological individualism" in social analysis. Sociology could not be based on a theory which took the individual as the starting-point of analysis, as in utilitarian philosophy. This was a "pre-social" individual who did not exist in reality. The individual was penetrated by society, i.e. "socialized". It was the social factors and the processes by which they penetrated and constrained the individual that constituted the distinctive subject-matter of sociology. This emphasis was extremely valuable in asserting the distinctiveness and importance of sociology. However, it also entailed some exaggerations and ambiguities in Durkheim's formulations. He was able to critize economics for proceeding as though the individual was motivated solely by egoistic desires, when in fact egoism might be a social product. But he himself operated with an *homo duplex* model of human nature, according to which man had two natures. According to this view sensations and sensory needs were necessarily egoistic because they originated in, and referred to, conditions of the biological organism. By contrast, conceptual thought and moral activity were "impersonal", or social products, because they did not belong to any particular person who used them. He never satisfactorily resolved the question of the sources of egoism — whether it was the biological, "pre-social" side of man, or a cultural (ideological) product.

To further complicate matters, it has to be pointed out that Durkheim was not "anti-individualist", as might be thought, simply on the basis of his opposition to methodological individualism. He was also opposed to the contrasting tradition of thought called "idealist holism", which was basically conservative in orientation and saw the relationship between the individual and society as being that of the microcosm of the whole. In this view the individuals should be like-minded imprints of the social mould. Durkheim had learned something from the positive side of utilitarian individualism, especially from the sociologist Herbert Spencer, to the effect that the position of the individual in modern society was different from that in traditional society. He was convinced that industrial society entailed specialization of functions, and that in this respect society had to cultivate individual differences and greater self-autonomy in individuals. Where he differed from the utilitarians was in his belief that the "cult of the individual" in modern society did not rest on egoistic pursuit of self-interest, but on the values that inspired the French Revolution, which were concerned with the dignity and worth of "man" in the abstract [3]. The ideals of this moral individualism meant that respect for the individual and the concomitant demand for equality became moral imperatives, entailing that the welfare and self-fulfilment of every member of society should be sought after.

Unfortunately, Durkheim's attack on methodological individualism and his desire to stress that sociology has a subject-matter of its own, which could not be explained by reference to individual or biological factors (such as race, instincts, passions, or drives), led him to overstate his case. In making a sharp distinction between social and individual facts he was led into conflating a number of different distinctions:

"(i) between the socially determined and the organically or bio-logically given;

(ii) between factors specific to particular societies, and abstracted or postulated features of 'human nature';

(iii) between factors that are general within a given society or group and those that are particular to one or several individuals;

(iv) between the experience and behaviour of associated individuals as opposed to those of isolated individuals;

(v) between socially prescribed obligations and spontaneous desires and behaviour;

(vi) between factors coming from 'outside' the individual and those generated within his consciousness;

(vii) between thoughts and actions directed towards social or public objects and those which are purely personal and private:

(viii) between altruistic and egocentric behaviour"[4].

However, despite this overstatement and the consequent blurring of some distinctions whilst he was illuminating others, Durkheim's forrceful assertion of the case for sociological explanation was essential if it was to succeed in establishing itself in the face of a great deal of ideological and academic opposition.

3.2.2 Sociology and its programme

Considering that Durkheim gained the reputation of being a fierce advocate of sociology, it is surprising to find that in his opening lecture in the first ever course of sociology in France, which he gave at Bordeaux in 1887, he adopted the most modest tone imaginable:

"Charged with the task of teaching a science born only yesterday, one which can as yet claim but a small number of principles to be definitively established, it would be rash on my part not to be awed by the difficulties of my task. . . .A young science should not be overly ambitious, and it enjoys greater credibility among scientific minds when it presents itself with greater modesty"[5] .

His anxiety, as he made clear, was that he was afraid of "awakening or reawakening in some of you the scepticism of which sociological studies have somethimes been the object." Such scepticism had been aroused by sociologists like Comte, who did not study specific societies, but produced a "philosophical meditation on human sociology in general." Sociology needed to draw in to its orbit specialists in specific areas of study, such as historians and students of law, who could gain from adopting a sociological perspective, and more importantly, who would supply the data which would enable sociology to practice its own "experimental" method of comparison. By comparing institutions, beliefs, and practices in different societies, sociology would be able to test hypotheses about their causes and functions.

Sociology had already made some progress in this direction as a result of the contributions of German scholars, such as Wagner and Schmoller in economics, and Ihering and Post in legal studies. As a result of their empirical studies and their reception into sociology it

"lost that erstwhile air of sudden improvization which had sometimes cast doubt upon its future. It no longer seemed to have miraculously appeared out of nowhere one sunny day. . . It has a clearly defined object and a method for studying it. The object consists of social facts. The method is observation and indirect experimentation, or, in other words, the comparative method" [5] , pp. 61-2.

In presenting this early outline of sociology, Durkheim said that there was one more thing that remained to be done and that was to subdivide the field into specialist areas, which would yield more specific questions to replace the over-broad questions that had been a feature of pre-scientific sociology. In this way it would attract better scholars and permit colaboration, in contrast to the past when a few philosophically minded scholars had taken it over and proceeded to

"mark it with their strong imprint to such an extent that it becomes their own property and seems to become confused with them. . .by becoming more specialized, science comes closer to things which are themselves specialized. It thus becomes more objective, more impersonal, and, consequently, accessible to the full range of individual talents and to all workers of good will"[5], p. 62.

This view of the virtue of scientific collaboration motivated him to start *l'Année sociologique*. By the time of his paper on "La sociologie" for the Exposition universelle et internationale de San Francisco in 1915 he was able to state with confidence and pride that this strategy of collaboration had succeeded: sociology had been divided into sub-areas, and specialist techniques and data had been brought in, whilst the general sociological perspective had brought a new sense of the social detetminants and interrelationships of specific phenomena. As he put it:

"The most urgent reform, therefore, was to bring sociology and these other special techniques closely together, to unite them in a fertile marriage, so as to give sociology the data it lacked, and, inversely, to bring the sociological idea down into these disciplines in such a manner as to make true social sciences of them. In order to assure this rapprochment and to make it more intimate, a periodical was established in 1896 under the name *Année sociologique*, whose aim is to glean from studies in the history of religion, the history of moral and legal institutions, moral statistics, and economic history, the facts that appear to be of particular interest to sociologists"[6].

As a result of these efforts Durkheim no longer felt it necessary to apologize for sociology's connection with Auguste Comte, but could state: "Comte is its father"[6], p. 378. Comte's main error had been to think that "he had not only founded sociology but had also completed it at the same time"[6], p. 379–80. But, said Durkheim, science is never completed:

"It consists of particular, restricted questions which bear on specific objects. Although these questions are interrelated, they must be treated separately; indeed their very interdependence appears only in so far as the science advances and to the extent to which it does. Consequently, sociology could not really become a positive science until it renounced its initial and over-all claim upon the totality of social reality. It had to introduce analysis and to distinguish ever more among parts, elements, and different aspects which could serve as subject matters for specific problems. It is to this task that the author of the present note has devoted himself with the help of a whole group of workers who have joined their efforts with his. Our ambition is to initiate for sociology what Comte called the era of specialization"[6], p. 380.

There is something to be said for approaching the question of Durkheim's conception of sociology from the direction of an appreciation of his work on *L'Année sociologique*. He himself saw that work as the fulfilment of his aspirations to put sociology on a scientific basis. Its mode of operation in terms of a division of labour, corresponding to main sub-areas and specialisms of sociology as he envisaged that subject, helps to explain why Durkheim's own sociology had certain gaps in it. For example, economics was an area that Durkheim said should be studied sociologically, and yet, as some critics have pointed out, Durkheim himself tended to neglect that area and gave little attention to economic factors. One reason for this was that, under the principle of division of labour in the team associated with *L'Année sociologique,* the sociology of economics was to be developed by other researchers (most notably, Francois Simiand). The idea was that these findings would eventually be fed back into general sociology and would then permeate other specialist areas where relevant. But in Durkheim's lifetime most progress was confined to developing the specialisms, and the task of building up general sociology on the basis of feedback from the specialized areas was neglected. In 1915 Durkheim could proudly list the achievements of the first stage of specialization, but there was little progress to report on the development of general sociology:

"Our ambition is to initiate for sociology what Comte called the era of specialization. A true division of labour has been instituted. Three groups of facts have been studied in particular: religious, moral and legal, and economic facts. And instead of carrying on general sociology, some of us have devoted ourselves to the sociology of religion, others to the sociology of morals and law, and still others to the sociology of economics. But even this division was much to general: within each of these special sociologies particular problems have been taken up — those of sacrifice and of magic by Henri Hubert and Marcel Mauss; *Les formes élementaires de la vie religiouse* and *Le suicide* by Durkheim; *La prohibition de l'inceste* and various studies of primitive marriage by the same author; *Le régime des castes* by Gélestin Bouglé; *Le salaire des ouvriere des mines* by Francois Simiand; and *La classe ouvriere et les niveaux de vie* by Maurice Halbwachs. More recently, an effort has been made to determine the social conditions upon which certain logical operations or certain forms of thought depend: we refer to the *Essai sur certaines formes primitives de classification* by Durkheim and Mauss, and the *Etude sur la représentation du temps* by Hubert" [6], p. 380.

This statement of the achievements of the Durkheimian school of sociology, made at the end of his life, gives a good indication of Durkheim's priorities. The first task had been to establish that sociology had a distinctive subject-matter, and this involved stressing that social phenomena had a reality of their own, *sui generis,* and they must be analysed by rigorous and objective methods of study. Thus, specialization and the development and demonstration of appropriate methods of analysis constituted the main priorities. The next task would be to combine these results in order to show the nature of the total social phenomenon and the general principles that ordered it; this was the task of general sociology:

"After analysis, there is need for synthesis, showing how those elements unite in a whole. Here is the justification of general sociology"[6], p. 374.

Unfortunately, Durkheim made less progress in developing general sociology, and there is no explicit general theory in Durkheimian sociology that could be compared with, for example, Marxist social theory. Durkheim's model, or general conception of the social whole, is similarly underdeveloped, although it can be pieced together. It entails going beneath the surface events of social life in order to discern the various levels of crystallization of social forces that constrain individuals' actions. It is this "going beneath the surface" that constitutes the first step in scientific analysis according to Durkheim:

"Instead of stopping at the exclusive consideration of events that lie at the surface of social life, there has arisen the need for studying the less obvious points at the base of it — internal causes and impersonal hidden forces that move individuals and collectivities" [6], p. 373.

It is these "impersonal hidden forces" that structure human action. In focusing on the search for structuring principles and processes, Durkheim gave his sociology its unmistakable "structuralist" character, which might be regarded as its most distinctive characteristic. (Certainly, it would be difficult to find any other theoretical or methodological characteristic that featured as prominently in the extremely varied works of the Durkheimian school, such as those listed above in Durkheim's account of the achievements of the team's intellectual division of labour.) The structuring principles and codes could be manifested in various forms and in varying degrees of crystallization. They could range from the highly crystallized forms of the spatial arrangement of dwellings, systems of communication and transport, and technologies, to the more codified types of rules such as those found in legal codes, and even to relatively uncrystallized currents of opinion. It was the constraining effect of these structures — crystallizations, rules, and codes — on individuals' actions, which made society possible, and at the same time, by making behaviour systematic, constituted it as a possible object of scientific investigation. It was for this reason that so much of Durkheim's sociology was taken up with things arranged as classifications, with discovering "the rule", and with the "type" and rate of social phenomena.

3.3 DEFINITIONS AND CONCEPTS

3.3.1 Sociology

Although Durkheim wrote a great deal about how things should be studied in sociology, and discussed many of the components of sociology, he never offered a comprehensive definition of sociology commensurate with the complex sociological model he employed. A successor of Durkheim's at the Sorbonne, Georges Gurvitch, attempted to reconstruct such a definition of Durkheimian sociology, and came up with the following complex formulation:

"Sociology is a science which studies, with an overall view, and in a typological and explanatory fashion, the different degrees of crystallization of social life, the base of which is found in states of the collective conscience, irreducible and opaque to individual consciences; these states are manifested in constraints, institutions, pressures, externally observable symbols, and materialized through transfiguration of the geographico-demographic surface, and at the same time these states of the collective conscience penetrate all these elements through the ideas, values, and ideals towards which the collective conscience inclines in the form of free currents of thought and aspiration" [7].

Durkheim himself offered two cryptic definitions of sociology. In the preface to the second edition of *The Rules of Sociological Method* he agreed with the formulation of two of his disciples, Mauss and Fauconnet, that,

"Sociology can then be defined as the science of institutions, of their genesis and of their functioning" [8].

By "institutions" he meant "all the beliefs and all the modes of conduct instituted by the collectivity" [8], p.13.

Earlier in the same work he had defined sociology as the study of social facts, which in turn were defined as follows:

"A social fact is every way of acting, fixed or not, capable of exercising on the individual an external constraint; or again, every way of acting which is general throughout a given society, while at the same time existing in its own right independent of its individual manifestations" [8], p. 13.

The character of sociology, as conceived by Durkheim, can also be deduced from the characterization he gave of its method and subject-matter. It was to be a science, and this entailed following certain rules. The first such rule was: "All preconceptions must be eradicated" [8], p. 31. By this he meant that all concepts originating outside science for unscientific needs should be avoided. Such lay concepts were "tyrranical", and the sociologist must "throw off, once and for all, the yoke of these empirical categories" [8], p. 32. A theoretical definition of the object to be studied was required:

"The first step of the sociologist ought to be to define the things he treats. . . A theory, indeed, can be checked only if we know how to recognize the facts of which it is intended to give an account" [8], p. 34.

The phenomenon to be studied should have some agreed external characteristics that make it recognizable to more than one person. Hence he defines the subject-matter of sociology as follows:

"The subject-matter of every sociological study should comprise a group of phenomena defined in advance by certain common external characteristics, and all phenomena so defined should be included within this group" [8], p. 35.

For example, certain acts have the external characteristic that they evoke from society the reaction called punishment, consequently, "We constitute them as a separate group, to which we give a common label; we call every punished act a crime, and crime thus defined becomes the object of a special science, criminology" [8], pp. 35-6.

According to Durkheim, fields of study which simply took over lay concepts and categories and allowed them to permeate the study with their prior values, were indulging in ideology. He gave as an example the economics of his day: "The ideological nature of economics is implied even in the expressions used by economists" [8], p. 25. The social facts that should constitute the subject-matter of sociology were not "factual" in the sense that they could be taken for granted as existing simply because everyone accepted them. They had to be theoretically constituted, or conceptualized.

3.3.2 Social facts and the model of the total social phenomenon

Durkheim's first rule for sociological analysis was: "Consider social facts as things"[8], p. 14. Today it seems odd that it should have been necessary to insist on the reality of social factors. Perhaps this is simply because we have learned the lesson that Durkheim was trying to teach, which is that there are constraining and determining factors of a social nature that must be taken into account in explaining human behaviour. In that respect, at least, we are all sociologists now. However, Durkheim had to contend against the prevalent tendency to reduce all explanation of human behaviour to the levels of individual psychology or biology — hence his emphasis on *social* facts. Secondly, by insisting that social *facts* were to be considered like things, he sought to persuade the sociologist to adopt the detached stance of the scientist and to approach all social phenomena with an open mind, setting aside all preconceptions and looking for empirical indicators of theoretically conceptualized factors operating beneath the surface of events. Sociology, as a science, could not be content with intuitive knowledge nor conventional wisdom about such things as economic practices, the State, suicide, and crime and punishment.

The characteristics of a social fact were: externality, constraint, and generality. A social fact had an existence external to any individual or the mind of any individual. It exercised a constraint over the individual in a number of ways, depending on its position on a continuum of social phenomena ranging from morphological facts that determined the availability of facilities, to the contraining force of norms backed by sanctions, to the constraints imposed by language, the force of myths and symbols, and the pressures of public opinion. Two modes of constraint can be distinguished among these various types of social factors: one is the constraint imposed by lack of choice, the other is the pressure to choose according to established notions of what ought to be the case. Morphological factors exercise the first kind of constraint, usually through the form and distribution of material resources. Institutions and collective representations, such as values, beliefs, and currents of opinions, are examples of the second kind of constraint. However, some social factors impose both kinds of constraint, a combination of material resource limitation and moral pressure to act in a certain way; an example might be the provision of single-sex accommodation for students by a university.

Durkheim's implicit model of the continuum of social phenomena, ranged in levels downwards from the surface level of the most crystallized down to the more obscure levels of the least crystallized phenomena, can be expressed as follows:

I. *Morphology (substratum)*
Volume, density and distribution of population. Territorial organization. Material objects incorporated in the society: buildings, channels of communication, monuments, technological instruments (e.g. machines, etc.).

II. *Institutions (normative sphere)*
II–A Formal rules and norms — expressed in fixed legal and sub-legal formulae, moral precepts, religious dogmas, political and economic forms, professional role definitions, — or in determining language conventions and the obligations of social categories.
II–B Informal rules and norms as applied in the preceding domains: customary models, collective habits and beliefs.

III. *Collective representations (symbolic sphere)*
III–A Societal values, collective ideals; opinions; representations which the society has of itself; legends and myths; religious representations (symbols, etc.).
III–B Free currents of social life, that are effervescent and not yet caught in a definite mould; creative collective thinking; values and representations in the process of emerging.†

†Adapted, with modifications and additions, from [9].

Fig. 3.1 – The multi-layered model of social phenomena (social facts).

Collective Representations and the Collective Conscience

The collective conscience, or common conscience, was defined as "The totality of beliefs and sentiments common to average citizens of the same society (which) forms a determinate system which has its own life"[10], p. 79. *Conscience,* in French, means both "consciousness" and "conscience", and so it always carries a certain ambiguity. The beliefs and sentiments that make up the collective conscience are moral and religious, according to the second sense, and cognitive in the first sense. The combination of the two senses in the French concept *conscience collective,* as used by Durkheim, gave it a significance and potency that was unrivalled in the rather sparse conceptual armoury of his early work. (At that stage the other major type of social fact was the "morphological", or material.) Indeed, Durkheim's eagerness to stress the potency and reality of the collective conscience invited the criticism that he believed in the existence of a group mind, which he denied. Nevertheless, although he seemed to refer to it as an integrated entity in his first book, *The Division of Labour,* it became simply a general category in the more conceptually developed later model of the social. It steadily gave way to the more discriminating concept "collective representations".

Durkheim began using the concept of collective representations in *Suicide,* when he wrote that "essentially social life is made up of representations", adding that "these collective representations are of quite another character from those of the individual"[11], p. 312. He wished to emphasize the collective or social origin and character of beliefs and ideas, as opposed to explanations which traced them to states of the individual consciousness. Collective representations included all "the ways in which the group conceives of itself in relation to objects which affect it"[8], p. xlix. They were derived from collective concerns: "The group differs from the individual in its constitution and the things that affect it are therefore of a different nature"[8]. Consequently, to understand the way in which a society thinks of itself and of its environment one must consider the nature of the society and not that of individuals. Even the symbols which express these conceptions change according to the type of society"[8].

The example Durkheim gives of this is the correspondence between totemic beliefs and clan organization. Furthermore, if the clan begins to believe in higher divinities it is likely that it has joined in a higher level of social organization, such as a tribe. He admitted one other possibility, and that was that once certain collective representations had come into existence they might proceed to develop in relative autonomy from material and morphological factors. In which case it might be found that there were certain rules of combination which were common to collective representations and the thought processes of the individual. If such rules could be found they would provide common ground for sociology and individual psychology; this was the task of social psychology. In fact, the most prominent claim to have followed up this suggestion has come from Claude Lévi-Strauss, who maintains that his structuralism follows up Durkheim's proposition that:

"Myths, popular legends, religious conceptions of all sorts, moral beliefs, etc., reflect a reality different from the individual's reality; but the way in which they attract and repel each other, unite or separate, may nevertheless be independent of their content and may depend uniquely on their general quality as representations. . . We need to investigate by comparison of mythical themes, popular legends, traditions, and languages, the manner in which social representations adhere to and repel one another, how they fuse or separate from one another, etc." [8] , p. l–li.

In summary, it can be seen that Durkheim made four claims for collective representations: (1) they are socially generated; (2) they represent social concerns; (3) there is a structural correspondence with social organization; (4) once formed they become relatively autonomous and combine, separate, and are transformed, according to their own laws.

Social Currents and the Group Mind

In trying to stress that social representations were something more than individual psychological phenomena, Durkheim sometimes made them sound like emanations from a group mind. This was particularly the case when he wrote about the least crystallized phenomona, which he called "social currents", and contrasted them with the more crystallized phenomena:

"But there are other facts without such crystallized form which have the same objectivity and the same ascendancy over the individual. These are called 'social currents'. Thus the great movements of enthusiasm, indignation, and pity in a crowd do not originate in any one of the particular individual consciousnesses. They come to each one of us from without and can carry us away inspite of ourselves" [8] , p. 4.

He used this notion of social currents as a major explanatory variable in Suicide. His argument, as we will see, was that suicide rates change as a result of changes in social currents:

"It is not mere metaphor to say of each human society that it has a greater or lesser aptitude for suicide; the expression is based on the nature of things. Each social group really has a collective inclination for the act, quite its own, and the source of all individual inclination, rather than their result. It is made up of the currents of egoism, altruism, or anomy running through the society under consideration with the tendencies to languorous melancholy, active renunciation, or exasperated weariness derivative from these currents. These tendencies of the whole social body, by affecting individuals, cause them to commit suicide"[11], pp. 299-300.

Although he said he was not using a mere mataphor, the notion of social currents does seem to draw on an electrical analogy, and this, combined with his almost exaggerated insistence on the reality of social facts, gave the impression that he believed in the existence of a group mind. It is now possible to see that what he was trying to express in his concept of social currents was the idea of a set of meanings that are shared (although not fixed) intersubjectively by members of a population. As these meanings change, and the changed meanings are communicated from one member to another, a change in the suicide rate (and in other rates) will occur.

Institutions

Durkheim understood by the concept "institution" a set of beliefs and practices that had become normative (obligatory) and that were focused on a recurrent or continuous social concern. As part of his polemic against Utilitarianism he stressed that institutions could not be explained simply as the rational arrangements contrived by individuals to deal with contingencies of existence. Institutions might well sustain the lives of individuals, but it could not be assumed that individuals set about establishing them with that end in view. He condemned Herbert Spencer and those other social theorists who had produced a number of specific theories on the basis of this assumption that institutions arose so as to permit individuals to attain their ends or express their nature, and who then went on to explain the development of the institutions as having the objective of making this expression easier or more complete:

"Thus domestic organization is commonly explained by the sentiment parents have for their children, and children for their parents; the institution of marriage, by the advantages it presents for the married pair and their progeny; punishment, by the anger which every grave attack upon his interests causes in the individual. All economic life, as economists of the orthodox school especially conceive and explain it, is definitely dependent upon a purely individual factor, the desire for wealth"[8], p. 100-101.

Durkheim denied that the structure of institutions could be explained by starting with the purposes in the minds of individuals (especially as these were difficult to discover), nor could they be explained simply in terms of their usefulness to the individual or society. He poured scorn on this utilitarian logic, asking sarcastically about the social utility of institutions that prolonged the lives of "imbeciles, idiots, lunatics, incurables of all sorts, of no use at all, yet whose existence is prolonged, thanks to the privations imposed upon the normal, healthy workers" [10], p. 416.

Institutions were such complex bodies of norms that they could only be explained in terms of their relations with other sets of social facts, e.g. as expressions of collective representations (such as values and symbols to which people are deeply attached) or as determined by morphological factors (such as technology, material resources, territory, pattern of settlement, demography). Morphological factors were ultimately decisive in determining which of the alternative sets of practices bearing on a given activity were progressively eliminated and which set became institutionalized. A more proximate selective determinant of which set of practices became institutionalized was that of the requirement for compatibility — the necessity for each institution to fit in with other institutions.

Although purpose and usefulness could not explain why a set of practices first became institutionalized, Durkheim did include usefulness among the explanatory factors for explaining the continuing functions of an institution. He chose the word "function" to characterise such usefulness because it did not carry the psychological connotations of "purpose" or "goal". He recommended that the sociologist should first search for the causes of an institution becoming established (by reference to other sets of social facts — collective representations and morphological factors), and then proceed to discover its function(s) and social usefulness:

"If the determination of function is thus to be delayed, it is still necessary for the complete explanation of the phenomena. Indeed, if the usefulness of a fact is not the cause of its existence, it is generally necessary that it be useful in order that it may maintain itself" [8], p. 97.

However, there could be exceptions to this methodological prescription, because some institutional practices could lose their functions and become survivals ("fossils"), or change their functions:

". . . a fact can exist without being at all useful, either because it has never been adjusted to any vital end or because, after having been useful, it has lost all utility while continuing to exist by the inertia of habit alone. There are, indeed, more survivals in society than in biological organisms. There are even cases where a practice or a social institution changes its function without thereby changing its nature"[8], p. 91.

As institutions developed they tended to become internally more differentiated and elaborated, and at the same time self-sustaining and self-justifying, i.e. the tendency is for institutions to become relatively more autonomous of the original set of factors that brought them into existence. The component elements develop a dynamism of their own. Consequently, institutions do not necessarily change concomitantly with changes in the morphological factors that brought them into being. As the institution becomes more independent of the morphological factors it also loses some of the close affinity it had with other institutions. These considerations concerning the relative autonomy of instituitions in relation to morphological factors and other institutions have particular relevance to any comparison between the different sociological models and theories of change in the work of Durkheim and Marx. Durkheim refused to give any privileged status to economic factors (whether morphological economic factors, such as technology, or institutional factors relating to the mode of production).

The *operation* of norms is explained by Durkheim in terms of two processes: (1) the influence of positive or negative sanctions that are structural components of the norm; and (2) the legitimating effect produced by the prestige of the collective representations that give the norm an appearance of coming from a superior source standing above the individual.

The first type of compulsion — sanctions of punishment and reward — is more of a factual or technical constraint because it entails calculation, and consequently it is not discussed much by Durkheim, except in *The Division of Labour* and with regard to crime and punishment. He had a greater theoretical interest in the second type of compulsion — that of a moral nature. He was fascinated by the way in which we internalize norms so that they become our own, and yet have an authority over us that gives us the sense that they come from a superior source (God, Society, the State, etc.) outside ourselves, in contrast with utilitarian calculation of advantage, and instincts, which are wholly *within* us. The reason for this is that the norms consist of collective representations, which have a social source, and which originally became fused into institutional practices in the course of social interactions in which the sense of reciprocal belonging was brought to a high pitch. The prototype of this was the religious gathering in which the participants were moved to feel part of a collective whole, and collective representations and practices associated with that experienced whole took on a *sacred* character, as opposed to the mundane world of everyday activity. Everyday activities were character-ized by technical and calculative activities, and constituted a profane sphere. This distinction, or contrast, between the sacred and profane was to feature in his discussion of religion, which he regarded as the prototype social institution [12]. The collective sense of respect for religious norms, due to their sacred character, closely paralleled the prestige enjoyed by all norms. High prestige collective representations, such as sacred myths, were to be found maintaining the sense of obliga-tion in religious institutions, and similarly, myths and symbols provided the sense of respect for norms in other institutions. The possible exception was with regard to economic norms, where there tended to be a greater degree of calculation of private interests. But even this predominantly mundane activity had once been related to the sacred sphere, and still in modern society certain economic norms were obeyed because they were ideologically justified by reference to superior authority of a "sacred" nature, e.g. religiously originated ethics of duty and vocation.

There is one final point to note in Durkheim's discussion of the constraining effects of social facts or institutions, and that concerns the scope left for the individual to modify these phenomena. He explained the possibilities and limits in this way:

"We do not mean to assert, incidentally, that social practices or beliefs enter into individual without undergoing variations — to say this would be to deny the facts. When we turn our thoughts to collective institutions — or rather, when we assimilate them — we individualize them, just as when we think of the sensible world, each of us colours it according to his gifts so that we see a great many different subjects, differently expressed and adapting themselves differently to the same physical milieu. This is why every one of us, up to a certain point, forms his own religious faith, his own cult, his own morality, and his own technology. There is no social uniformity which does not accommodate a whole scale of individual gradations; there is no collective fact which imposes itself on all individuals uniformly. Nevertheless, the area of variations that are possible and tolerated is always and everywhere more or less restricted. Almost absent in the religious and moral sphere, where innovation and reform are for all practical purposes always called delinquent or sacrilegious, this area is more extensive in the sphere of economic phenomena. But sooner or later, we encounter, even here, a limit that we cannot transcend.

Hence the characteristic feature of social facts lies in the ascendancy which they exert over the minds of individuals"[6], p. 367-8.

Social Morphology (Substratum)

In setting aside a specific section of *L'Année sociologique* to deal with works on social morphology, Durkheim described its subject-matter in the following way:

"Social life rests upon a substratum which is determinate both in its extent and in its form. It is composed of the mass of individuals who comprise the society, the manner in which they are disposed upon the earth, and the nature and configuration of objects of all sorts which affect collective relations. Depending on whether the population is more or less sizable, more or less dense; depending on whether it is concentrated in cities or dispersed in the country-side; depending on the way in which the cities and houses are constructed; depending on whether the space occupied by the society is more or less extensive; depending on the borders which define its limits, the avenues of communication which traverse it, and so forth, this social stratum will differ"[13].

The study of these phenomena was being undertaken by various disciplines, and they needed to be drawn together. He mentioned geography, which studied the territorial forms of nations, history, which retraced the evolution of rural or urban groups; and demography, which covered all that concerned the distribution of population. Their findings, which should be explanatory and not just descriptive, would provide an account of the anatomical structure of ways of life in the social realm, as the study of anatomy did in the life sciences.

In his various discussions of the development of institutions Durkheim suggested that morphological factors played a major deter-mining role in the genesis of institutions, but that this declined in later stages, when other social factors come to exercise a more immediate or direct influence. From this it can be seen that he was not averse to giving a materialist explanation, like Marx, where it was appropriate.

Crystallization and Consolidation

The difference between the various levels of social phenomena was expressed by Durkheim in terms of degrees of crystalization or consolid-ation. The level of morphological phenomena was described as "ways of existing". These ways of existing were nothing more than crystallized "ways of acting". The degrees of crystallization ranged from the most crystallized, such as territorial divisions and patterns of habitation, through institutions, and down to the dynamic and fluid collective representations, such as fashions and currents of opinion:

"There is thus a whole series of degrees without a break in continuity between the facts of the most articulated structure and those free currents of social life which are not yet definitely moulded. The differences between them are, therefore, only differences in the degree of consolidation they present. Both are simply life, more or less crystallized" [8], p. 12.

Normal and Pathological Facts

As the various levels of social phenomena were interrelated and inter-penetrating, Durkheim believed it should be possible to construct a series of typical sets, which could be arranged along an evolutionary or developmental continuum. At each point on the continuum certain social facts would be "normal", and any deviations could be considered "pathological":

"A social fact is normal, in relation to a given social type at a given phase of its development, when it is present in the average society of that species at the corresponding phase of its evolution" [8], p. 64.

Thus, crime was not necessarily "pathological", which might be the commonsense assumption, but rather certain crimes and rates of crime were perfectly normal in a given social type, but other types and rates of crime could be considered "pathological". Unfortunately, this kind of typologizing or modelling, when dependent on a limited number of historical cases, is very hard to carry out, and it runs the risk of sinking into value judgements about "healthy" and "unhealthy" social phenomena. Furthermore, it is almost impossible to apply to existing, ongoing societies, which tended to be referred to as "transitional" by Durkheim because they had not yet reached the state that his theoretical projection of the evolutionary process posited as normal. As with most theories that contain an evolutionary element, there was an element of wishful-thinking in his belief that contemporary conflicts and social problems were simply part of a transitional crisis before the emergence of a more healthy state.

The Study of Social Facts in Durkheim's Main Works

In order to gain an idea of how Durkheim uses the concept of a social fact we can briefly outline the structure of his argument in the three major works: *Division of Labour, Suicide,* and *Elementary Forms of the Religious Life.* In each work the argument is arranged in three parts. First, he gives a definition of the subject-matter. Secondly, he presents various suggested explanations of this phenomenon, usually of a psychologistic or individualistic nature. He then uses a combination of argument and data to show the inadequacy of these explanations, as, for example, with Spencer's thesis that the division of labour results from the pursuit of increased happiness, that suicide rates are explicable in terms of insanity, and that religion can be seen as the outgrowth of natural or cosmic forces. Finally, in each case he puts forward his own sociological explanation in which the social fact in question, the growth in the division of labour, the comparative rates of suicide, totemic beliefs and practices, are explained in terms of other social facts. In the *Division of Labour* the growth in population volume, population density, and then in "moral density", produces a growth in social differentiation, the division of labour, and the emergence of organic solidarity. In *Suicide* the comparative rates of suicide are determined by different suicidogenic currents, which are themselves the result of religious and political values in the society. While in the *Elementary Forms,* he argues that religion serves certain functional needs that bind people together, and that what people worship is really society itself.

REFERENCES

[1] Robert A. Nisbet, *Emile Durkheim*, Englewood Cliffs, New Jersey, Prentice-Hall, 1965.

[2] Ginsberg, *On the Diversity of Morals*, London, Heinemann, 1956, p. 51.

[3] Anthony Giddens, "The 'Individual' in the writings of Emile Durkheim", in *European Journal of Sociology*, 12, 2, 1971, pp. 210-28.

[4] Steven Lukes, *Emile Durkheim: His Life and Work*, Harmondsworth, Penguin, 1975, pp. 20-1.

[5] Durkheim, "Course in Sociology: Opening Lecture", in Mark Traugott (ed.), *Emile Durkheim on Institutional Analysis*, Chicago, University of Chicago Press, 1978, pp. 43-4.

[6] Durkheim, "Sociology", in Kurt H. Wolff (ed.), *Emile Durkheim et al., Essays on Sociology and Philosophy*, New York, Harper Torchbook edn., 1964, 376-85, p. 381.

[7] Georges Gurvitch, *Traité de sociologie*, Paris, Presses Universitaires de France, 1958, 2nd edn. 1962, p. 11, my translation.

[8] *The Rules*, 1938, p. lvi.

[9] Jean Claude Filloux's introduction to Emile Durkheim, *Les Science Sociale et l'action*, Paris, Presses Universitaires de France, 1970, p. 48.

[10] *Division of Labour*, p. 79.

[11] *Suicide*, p. 312.

[12] Cf. G. Poggi, "The Place of Religion in Durkheim's Theory of Institutions", *European Journal of Sociology, 12*, 2, 1971, pp. 229–60.

[13] Durkheim, "Note on Social Morphology", originally published in *L'Année sociologique, 2*, (1897–98), 520–21; the quotation is from Traugott (ed.), 1978, p. 88.

3.4 THE DIVISION OF LABOUR IN SOCIETY

3.4.1 Content, Context and Argument of the Book

On a first reading, *The Division of Labour in Society* [1] seems the most dated and least convincing of Durkheim's major works. However, it is important for understanding the starting-point of his sociology and its subsequent course of development. It also contains many of the main components of his sociological model and method. In addition, the famous second preface, published in 1902, 'Some Remarks on Occupational Groups', sets out his suggestions for dealing with the pathological tendencies of capitalist social organization.

Although Durkheim wrote within the evolutonary framework of his sociological predecessors, Comte and Spencer (and even Marx), his problematic — the system of questions he addressed — was different in some respects. His predecessors had been mainly concerned with the contrast between feudal society and its successor, capitalist society. Durkheim's problematic was directed at a deeper level, or a longer term perspective, and concerned the relation of the individual to society. The developments he discussed were related not simply to the changing social relations brought about by capitalism, but to change in the bases of social solidarity that began to occur in the most primitive or ancient societies. This is illuminated by the fact that most of his examples are drawn from societies such as the American Indians, the Jewish tribes of the Old Testament, ancient Egypt, and the Roman Republic. (In his later work, *The Elementary Forms of the Religious Life,* he was to take most of his examples from ethnographic reports on the Australian aborigines.) It is the relationship between the individual and society that constituted the problematic of all aspects of Durkheim's work, as manifested in the specific sociological, moral and political problems it chose to address. The main sociological problem was concerned with demonstrating the existence of society as a reality distinct from its individual parts, and composed of layers of social structures and social forces that moulded and constrained the individual. The moral problem was how to reconcile individual freedom and social order. The political problem was how to foster forms of social organization that would produce spontaneous solidaristic tendencies and maximize individual freedom.

The subject-matter of the book is clearly set out in the preface to the first edition:

"This work had its origins in the question of the relations of the individual to social solidarity. Why does the individual, while becoming more autonomous, depend more upon society? How can he be at once more individual and more solidary?" The answer, he says, lies in "a transformation of social solidarity due to the steadily growing development of the division of labour"[1], pp. 37-38.

The questions are clear enough, but to a present-day reader the framework may be obscure. Just what is the framework and its associated concepts that we are expected to have as a resource for understanding these questions? Durkheim insists that discussion be carried on in a scientific form, and he rejects all lay conceptualizations. Fortunately, he makes clear in his introduction the sources of the issues and the concepts. He mentions that several thinkers from the earliest times had seen the importance of the division of social labour (Aristotle is specificially mentioned), but Adam Smith, at the end of the eighteenth century, was the first to attempt a theory of it. The empirical reality to which the theory referred had become obvious to everyone by the end of the nineteenth century:

"Nowadays, the. phenomenon has developed so generally it is obvious to all. We need have no further illusions about the tendencies of modern history; it advances steadily towards powerful machines, towards great concentrations of forces and capital, and consequently to the extreme division of labour. Occupations are infinitely separated and specialized, not only inside the factories, but each product is itself a speciality dependent upon others"[1], p. 39.

Durkheim notes that the concept of the division of labour had become part of the accepted wisdom, although ideas about it had not advanced much since Adam Smith, despite its frequent use by economists. There had been two developments, however. One was the broadening of the scope of the notion as a result of the work of biologists, who had demonstrated that the more specialized the functions of an organism, the greater its development. The result was to give the concept a wider, evolutionary meaning: "The division of labour in society appears to be no more than a particular form of this general process"[1], p. 41. This, in turn, had led to another development in discussions of the concept, and that was a debate about the moral merits of the division of social labour.

Is specialization good or bad? Some people made it into a moral imperative, saying "Make yourself usefully fulfil a determinate function" [1], p. 43. Others pointed to the degrading nature of the division of labour in its effect on workers. For his part, Durkheim recommended the avoidance of moral assertions, and advocated the sociological analysis of the phenomenon, which he equated with an attempt to get at the empirical facts of the matter. Analysis was to be divided into three parts; first, an attempt should be made to determine the function of the division of labour — what social need it satisfied; second, we should then determine the causes and conditions on which it is dependent; and third, we should try to classify the principal deviant, or abnormal forms that it takes. Summarized in modern terms, these three Durkheimian modes of analysis are: functional analysis, causal analysis, and the ideal type analysis (or modelling).

Such is Durkheim's introductory outline of the issues and his approach. It emerges only later that the thesis has certain adversaries in mind as principal intellectual opponents, against whom its arguments are directed. The opponents are of two sorts. On the one hand there are the proponents of traditional moral philosophy, who believe all questions of ethics can be resolved by deduction from *a priori* principles. On the other hand are ranged social philosophies which take the individual's inherent needs and capacities as their starting point, and so reduce all social questions to questions of individual psychology. In the first camp were Catholic moral philosophers and conservative traditionalists. In the second camp were Utilitarian philosophers and political economists, the most prominent of these being also the most influential sociologist of the nineteenth century — Herbert Spencer.

It could be said that the main scholarly intention of Durkheim's work was to call into question all assertions about society that had not been framed in a form that permitted empirical testing, and to advocate the formulation of questions in sociological terms that gave pride of place to social factors as opposed to individual psychological or biological factors. He shared the conviction of the moralists that morals, interpreted in a very broad sense, constituted a fundamental layer of social existence that was indispensable for society, but he insisted that the subject be brought down to earth and the morals be studied by way of their concrete manifestations, particularly with regard to sanctions against their contravention. Empirical and comparative investigation could reveal the precise nature of moral codes and their social conditions of existence. In this way it should be possible to explain why certain codes exist in specific social conditions, as in the case of the large number of moral injunctions safeguarding the rights and possessions of the individual in the societies of industrial capitalism. In this, as in many other points, Durkheim's sociology had an impact on some contemporaries that was very similar to that of Marx's mode of analysis. The impact was that of a seemingly radical relativization of moral and legal codes, and of their ideological justifications. Although Durkheim's own moral and political preferences creep back in, he is much less inclined than earlier sociologists, such as Spencer, to give the impression that society has steadily evolved until it has reached its highest level in his own present society. Indeed, the third part of his book is given over to portraying the existing society as being very poorly regulated and with a forced or artificial division of labour that left society in a pathological state.

3.4.2 Spencer and social evolution

Spencer's sociology exerted a great influence in the second half of the nineteenth century, and there are at least forty references to him in *The Division of Labour*. His combination of social evolutionary doctrines and utilitarian philosophical principles made up a potent intellectual force, buttressed by the prestige of Darwin's theory of evolution and advances in biological sciences, and the ideological requirements of competitive capitalism, with its emphasis on individual striving and the sanctity of individual property rights and the individual as consumer. However, towards the end of the century these principles began to appear inadequate as a basis for national unity and progress, espcially in France, which had suffered defeat at the hands of Germany and found its prospects for progress blocked by social divisions.

The most widely-canvassed alternative to the *laissez-faire* principles of Spencer and economists of the so-called Manchester School was an approach which expected the State to create social solidarity and to direct social progress. This was the approach favoured by a number of theorists, such as Comte in France, and many of those whose work Durkheim had encountered in Germany, including Ferdinand Tönnies. Although Durkheim's ideas on social development followed a similar line to Comte and the Germans, he differed from them in significant respects on this issue. On practical political grounds he did not think much of the political regimes that were likely to result from their approach, such as Bonapartist authoritarianism, or State directed capitalism (which was Tönnies' version of socialism). On sociological grounds he maintained that industrial society, in its occupational structure, contained the basis for a realistic, organic solidarity, that represented a superior basis for social integration than either self-interest or mechanical solidarity imposed by the State. Although using a similar sort of classification of societies along a developmental continuum, from simple to complex forms, with "mechanical solidarity" at one end and "organic solidarity" at the other, his emphasis was on the capacity of levels of social organization below that of the State for producing solidarity. He was as realistic as Marx in seeing that the economic structures were the dominant structures of industrial society, but he also believed they had to be more than just economic if they were to produce social stability and integration. In effect, they had to accentuate their moral capacities, and their potential for enabling the individual to feel a positive attachment to society.

Durkheim's discussion of the development of the division of labour, by its very use of that key-note term, was bound to place him within the framework of the social evolutionary paradigm. This created problems for him because, when trying to differentiate his position from others, such as Spencer, who wrote about the division of labour, he had to struggle against the priorities imposed by that paradigm. For example, the concept of the division of labour carried the implication that economic factors were the most fundamental. But Durkheim believed that "the claim sometimes advanced that in the division of labour lies the fundamental fact of all social life is wrong". Instead, his sociological model had shared beliefs and sentiments as its most fundamental level, i.e. the collective conscience.

"There is, then, a social life outside the whole division of labour, but which the latter presupposes. That is, indeed, what we have directly established in showing that there are societies whose cohesion is essentially due to a community of beliefs and sentiments, and it is from these societies that those whose unity is assured by the division of labour have emerged"[1], p. 277.

In Durkheim's eyes it was manifestly not the case, contrary to the confident assertion of Spencer and utilitarian philosophy, that social solidarity was produced automatically be each individual pursuing his own interests in economic exchange. Durkheim pointed out that economic exchanges in the modern division of labour were based on contracts, and contracts required a prior, moral framework, and that framework could not be explained as a product of exchange. Furthermore, Durkheim repudiated the evolutionist theory that made individual interest (egoism) the starting point of human history and pictured cooperation and sociability (altruism) as a recent historical phenomenon. He expressed regret that the prestige of Darwin's evolutionary ideas had given this hypothesis authority, and had resulted in the drawing of a grotesque contrast between primitive societies in which egoism was suppressed by coercion, whilst modern society could depend upon the spirit of altruism emerging spontaneously among its members. It was not necessary to combat reactionary philosophies that imagined a paradise lost in the past by making past society appear dreary and by systematically belittling it. Nor was it scientific to dismiss evidence of altruistic ideas in past societies as nothing more than superstitions. Durkheim's view of human nature was that it contained a dualism. Every individual had egoistic and altruistic tendencies, and the existence of society depended on the maintenance of a certain degree of altruism. However, in contrasting primitive and advanced societies, Durkheim believed we would find that the proportion and content of these tendencies, as incorporated in culture, had changed.

3.4.3 Structure and change in primitive societies
Durkheim's main theoretical interest was in the functioning and content of the collective conscience and collective representations which encompassed much of what modern sociology calls *Culture,* especially those aspects of culture that have an obligatory character, deviance from which brings into play sanctions typical of a society at that particular stage of development. All levels of culture were structured, or codified, and the codes could be deciphered by the sociologists. So far as the collective conscience was concerned, its contents could be most easily observed in the form of legal codes, as these were the most highly formalized codes, with the most clearly specified sanctions. In the simpler societies, characterized by a low division of labour, and where, as a result, there was a high degree of resemblance and low differentiation in the functions performed by members of the society, the law was repressive. Any infringement of the mechanical solidarity produced by resemblance was highly disturbing and so severely punished.

The simpler societies tended to be small, with everyone experiencing the same conditions of existence, and therefore having the same perspective, which was concrete and local in its characteristic ideas (representations):

"In a small society, since everyone is clearly placed in the same conditions of existence, the collective environment is essentially concrete. It is made up of beings of all sorts who fill the social horizon. The states of conscience representing it then have the same character. First, they are related to precise objects, as this animal, this tree, this plant, this natural force, etc"[1], p. 287.

Religion is the typical form of the collective conscience in the simpler societies, and it too is concrete and local in its representations, concerned with beings that relate to animals, trees, plants, and natural forces. Social organization is also simple and local, and its typical form is segmental, according to which all portions or groups are based on resemblance rather than difference. The horde is the ideal type of an undifferentiated society, and then there is the clan form of segmental organization, which is a horde that has ceased to be independent by becoming an element in a more extensive group.

Despite the primacy of the culture factors in providing the basis for sociability, and constituting, in Durkheim's model of the total social phenomenon, the fundamental level, in *The Division of Labour* it is to material factors that he looks for explaining change and development. The thesis of the book is that functional specialization is brought about by an increase in material and "moral" density. By these terms he means increases in population density and in social interaction and exchange. The growth of cities is the "characteristic symptom" of this phenomenon. Durkheim's account of the "progressive condensation" of societies in historical development draws heavily on Spencer's discussion in his *Principles of Sociology,* particular with reference to the importance of the population factor, involving an increase in volume and density of population, in bringing about an increase in the division of labour. Increased population density, the growth of cities, and improvements in transport and communication, all give rise to increased condensation of society, by multiplying intra-social relations. He speaks of the gaps between the segments being filled in by the growth of interactions and interdependence as individuals and groups specialize in serving certain functions and depending on others for what they cannot produce themselves.

Durkheim admitted that it was not possible to observe any existing society that corresponded to his model of the most basic social organization, the horde, but its prior existence could be postulated by the existence of societies which were formed out of a collection of simpler groups which approximated that type. The Indians of North America, particularly the Iroquois tribe, are given as an example. There was very little hierarchy or differentiation, and the segments were like the rings of an earthworm. These segmental societies with a clan base were a good example of societies in which there was a preponderance of mechanical solidarity; that is, solidarity derived from likeness. Members shared the same functions and perceptions, and religion pervaded the whole social life. Property was held in common, just as were beliefs. To act contrary to the collective conscience, defined as "the totality of beliefs and sentiments common to average members of the same society", was to risk being punished for having committed an offence against religion as well as against the whole society.

3.4.4 Law and Punishment

It is Durkheim's use of law and punishment as indicators of societies approximating to his models that constitutes perhaps the most original sociological contribution of *The Division of Labour*. (Another major contribution is his use of the concept of "anomie", which was to feature extensively in *Suicide*.) Examination of systems of crime and punishment serves several puposes in his sociological analysis. Its most important purpose is to provide an empirical indicator of the nature and condition of various levels of social organization and culture in a society, in keeping with his general sociological model. It also serves the polemical purpose of combating moral philosophers who insisted that there were absolute moral principles, from which emanated all laws and morals in different societies, and at the same time it combated the Utilitarians' assumption that moral behaviour was the result of individuals making agreements that would maximize their happiness. Durkheim aimed to show that there was no such thing as an intrinsically criminal act. What was defined as criminal depended completely on the pervailing sentiments and beliefs in each society. This follows naturally from his initial definition of a crime: "an act is criminal when it offends strong and defined states of the collective conscience"[1], p. 80. There was no single formula that would allow us to predict in advance what would be a crime; it would depend completely on the collective conscience at any time:

> "In other words, we must not say that an action shocks the common conscience because it is criminal, but rather that it is criminal because it shocks the common conscience. We do not reprove it because it is a crime, but it is a crime because we reprove it. As for the intrinsic nature of these sentiments, it is impossible to specify them. They have the most diverse objects and cannot be encompassed in a single formula. We can say that they relate neither to vital interests of society nor to a minimum of justice"[1], p. 81.

Law and the penal system provided an empirical indicator (an index external to individual subjectivity) of more obscure and less easily observed social phenomena at other levels of the social system, such as morals and currents of public opinion. In simpler societies, these more impenetrable levels were dominated by collective beliefs and sentiments of a religious nature, and so the law was in large part religious law. Infractions were immediately, passionately, and severely punished, because they were a threat to the basic solidarity of the society, which was based on sameness of the mentalities of members, whose minds were largely infused with the collective conscience. The function of the law was to repress deviance, and this repressive law reserved its most severe sanctions for offences against religious prescriptions, because these hit at the core of the collective conscience. According to Durkheim, the evidence showed that this relationship was so well established in primitive societies that they did not bother to spell out the details of punishments for such serious offences. Where records existed of punishments inflicted, as in the Old Testament, they showed that religious offences were the most seriously punished. Offences that modern societies consider grave, such as murder, were often less severely punished. Another characteristic of repressive law was that, although some of the sanctions may be specified, the moral beliefs or justifications were not. This was because everyone knew them, and there was no need for formalization. For example, the homicide law did not commend respect for life, but simply specified the punishment. Durkheim also rejected any explanations of punishment in terms of its deterrent value. If that had been the case, punishments would not be graded according to the seriousness of the crimes but according to the strength of motivation to commit them. The function of repressive sanctions was to reaffirm solidarity in society by taking vengeance on the offender. Durkheim then shocked his more complacent readers by asserting that this is still the case in modern societies as far as repressive sanctions, or the criminal law, is concerned. The difference is that "it now produces its effects with a much greater understanding of what it does". But despite this greater consciousness of cause and effects in the modern penal system, "the internal structure of phenomena remains the same, whether they be conscious of it or not". (This is an example of Durkheim's structuralist explanation and his rejection of explanation in terms of the conscious intentions of actors.) His conclusion is that "the essential elements of punishment are the same as of old. And in truth, punishment has remained, at least in part, a work of vengeance"[1], p. 88.

Durkheim's explanation of penal systems is functionalist and structuralist. Punishment serves the "unconscious" (or "latent") function of reaffirming elements of the collective conscience and so maintaining social solidarity. "Its true function is to maintain social cohesion intact, while maintaining all its vitality in the common conscience . . . We can thus say without paradox that punishment is above all designed to act upon upright people. . ."[1], p. 108. The increasingly more conscious, or intended, functions of penal policies, such as policies of correction and deterrence, were still only secondary in modern societies. This could be seen from the fact that penalties were graded according to the gravity of the offence, which meant the extent to which it offended the collective conscience, not according to the proven success of such penalties in reforming or deterring offenders. The more fundamental causes of penal codes were the functional requirements of deeper cultural structures, such as beliefs and sentiments. Penal codes derived from these deeper sentiments, and the functioning of these codes, reaffirmed and revitalized the sentiments, which provided the social solidarity based on the binding nature of the collective conscience.

The difference between law and punishment in primitive societies and in more complex societies was that the scope and character of the collective conscience had changed. Mechanical solidarity based on resemblance had decreased as the division of labour increased. Law and punishment provided an external index of the change. There was still some criminal law which, in its repressive sanctions, functioned to revitalize and reaffirm the collective conscience when it was offended directly, or when it was offended indirectly by actions against its representative organs, the State institutions, such as government agencies and regulations, or the police. Otherwise, law and punishment were concerned with restoring relations between individuals, or contractual parties, to the state in which they had existed before the act which upset them. In societies with an advanced division of labour there was less resemblance and more differences based on specialization of functions. Social solidarity depended on cooperation between specialized functions and their agents, and restitutive sanctions and civil law reflected these structural realities. The specialization of functions was most obviously apparent in commercial legal codes, which regulated business contracts. But restitutive law also included procedural law, administrative law, constitutional law, and domestic law, all of which were concerned with maintaining or restoring cooperative relations.

The extension of restitutive law and the diminution of repressive law was an index of an increase in the division of labour and the changed base of social solidarity. The reciprocity between specialized functions created an *organic* solidarity, analogous to the relations between specialized organs in the body. However, one of the organs had a certain priority because it directed the functioning of the others; in the body it is the brain, and in society that organ is the State. It was because of its centrality and representative nature that the State had a privileged position with regard to the law. Some crimes, which did not seem to offend directly against public opinion, were nonetheless severely punished, and this was because they damaged the dignity or authority of the State and its agencies, such as the police. The State laid claim to being the representative and embodiment of the collective conscience, and so any offence against the State was an offence against the collective conscience – thus constituting a threat to social solidarity. However, in terms of the evolutionary framework of Durkheim's models, such claims should diminish, as they amounted to basing solidarity in a society with an advanced division of labour on the mechanism of like-mindedness or a forced conformity, rather than on functional interdependence. Organic solidarity could only supplant mechanical solidarity in a society where all the parts – institutions, and role-players in institutions – functioned according to rules (norms) that were spontaneously generated and positively accepted. The problem with existing industrial capitalist societies in Durkheim's view was that such a situation had not been achieved, and the division of labour was artificial and forced. Consequently, there was widespread 'anomie' – an absence of recognized and positively accepted norms to regulate action, and in Marx's terms "alienation" due to "forced" division of labour.

3.4.5 Anomie and the forced division of labour

According to Durkheim, the prevalence of anomie, which he was to document further in his study of suicide, showed that the line of development of the division of labour had deviated from its "logical" course. The current line of development taken by the existing industrial/capitalist societies seemed to him to be "abnormal" or "pathological", because it deviated from the path of developing organic solidarity. The third section of the book is given over to an examination of these pathological developments, which he suggested were due to an over-rapid industrialization and unequal distribution of power between the groups or classes involved. Inequality was particularly evident in the relations between classes, because those who had only their labour to offer were in a weaker position when entering into a contract than those who had the accumulated resources to purchase their labour, especially in conditions in which inheritance of wealth perptuated inequality:

"If one class of society is obliged, in order to live, to take any price for its services, while another can abstain from such action thanks to resources at its disposal which, however, are not necessarily due to any social superiority, the second has an unjust advantage over the first at law. In other words, there cannot be rich and poor at birth without there being unjust contracts" [1], p. 384.

Organic solidarity could develop only if there was a progressive elimination of external inequalities in the conditions affecting contracting partners. Inherited wealth was one major source of inequality that would have to be abolished. Other external inequalities that needed to be eliminated were those which hindered the "spontaneous" division of labour; by which he meant all those factors which prevented people from entering the occupations for which they were best suited. In short, he believed equality of oportunity was required to produce organic solidarity in a society with an advanced division of labour:

". . . we may say that the division of labour produced solidarity only if it is spontaneous and in proportion as it is spontaneous. But by spontaneity we must understand not simply the absence of all express violence, but also of everything that can even indirectly shackle the free unfolding of the social force that each carries in himself. It supposes, not only that individuals are not relegated to determinate functions by force, but also that no obstacle, of whatever nature, prevents them from occupying the place in the social framework which is compatible with their faculties. In short, labour is divided spontaneously only if society is constituted in such a way that social inequalities exactly express natural inequalities" [1], p. 377.

Inequalities external to the individual's inherent capacities resulted in a "forced" division of labour that affected whole classes. This was different from the "anomic" division of labour, which referred to an absence of regulation of the relations between functions and classes. The anomic division of labour also manifested itself in conflict between classes, especially in disputes over wages, whenever there was no mechanism for reaching agreement. However, Durkheim's discussion of the class conflict associated with the forced division of labour showed that he did not think the mere absence of regulations, as in anomic division of labour, was the main problem:

"It is not sufficient that there be rules, however, for sometimes the rules themselves are the cause of evil. This is what occurs in class-wars. The institution of classes and of castes constitutes an organization of the division of labour, and it is a strictly regulated organization, although it often is a source of dissention. The lower classes not being, or no longer being, satisfied with the role which has devolved upon them from custom or by law aspire to functions which are closed to them and seek to dispossess those who are exercising those functions. Thus civil wars arise which are due to the manner in which labour is distributed"[1], p. 374.

His discussion of the need to remove the inequalities which produce the forced division of labour rather than a meritocracy based on inherent talent and preference, shows that his main concern was with social equality. It is true that some of his criticisms were directed against the inefficient or insufficient regulation of the existing socio-economic system, which included the failure to regulate markets and to plan the economy, and "abnormal" division of labour due to inefficient organization. But his view of what would constitute a "normal" state amounted to more than a more efficiently regulated version of the existing system; it involved projecting structural tendencies of past development beyond the existing state and towards an ideal state of greater equality. The main task of an advanced society was not to improve efficiency, but to strive for justice.

"The task of the most advanced societies is, then, a work of justice. That they, in fact, feel the necessity of orienting themselves in this direction is what we have already shown and what everyday experience proves to us. Just as the ideal of lower societies was to create or maintain as intense a common life as possible, in which the individual was absorbed, so our ideal is to make social relations always more equitable, so as to assure the free development of all our socially useful forces. . . . There are no needs more firmly entrenched than these tendencies, for they are a necessary consequences of changes which have occurred in the structure of societies"[1], p. 387-8.

By the end of *The Division of Labour*, it is clear that Durkheim had doubts about the possibility of organic solidarity emerging automatically from the increasing division of labour. It would require a more conscious effort of planning and reform to bring it about. It was to this end that he added his suggestions for the developing of occupational associations, as set out in the *Second Preface*, and also insisted that social causes of inequality should be eliminated. In contrast to Spencer, the Utilitarians, and most nineteenth century economists, Durkheim's social analysis led to the advocacy of more 'collectivist' social policies. The anomic and abnormal forms of the division of labour could only be solved by more planning of the economy, better organization, and more organized involvement of workers and employers in the joint regulation of their industries.

3.4.6 Individualism

The issue of individualism reappears frequently with regard to two types of development. Firstly, he traces the development of "individuation", whereby there is a loosening of the bonds that bind the individual in the collectivity. In contrast with simple societies, advanced societies exhibit a lower volume, intensity, and rigidity of the beliefs, values, and rules of conduct that constitute the collective conscience. This process can be described as "individuation" because it leaves individuals with a greater scope to develop their own propensities and inclinations. But this does not mean that the collective conscience disappears, which would run counter to Durkheim's fundamental view of society as a cultural unity. Rather, the content of the collective conscience changes and is typically different from that of simple societies. Secondly, therefore, Durkheim discusses individualism in terms of changes in the content of the culture of advanced societies compared with that of the simpler societies. The typical moral ideal or ideology of the culture of advanced societies is that of the "cult of the individual", according to Durkheim. This can take many forms, and can co-exist with different types of economic arrangements, but it always entails a moral validation of the specialized division of labour, and from that there follows the concomitant belief that individuals should be able to develop their talents and capacities to the fullest extent. This value was expressed in the slogan of the French Revolution: "Liberty, equality and fraternity", and was fully endorsed by Durkheim as the appropriate value for modern societies based on an advanced division of labour.

The theory of change

The theory of change employed in *The Division of Labour* focuses on the interplay between material and ideal factors. It starts with material factors − that is, changes in the volume and density of the raw material of society. An increase in the degree of concentration of the social mass (population increases, urbanization, improved communications and transport) produces higher levels of social interaction. This engenders competition and conflict, which in turn gives rise to differentiation of functions, the division of labour, on which organic solidarity is based. However, although this occurs in a seemingly 'mechanical' fashion, determined by structural pressures, it does not inevitably take this course unless certain cultural factors facilitate it [1], p. 286. Among these so-called "secondary factors" are a change in the content of the common conscience from the local and concrete to more abstract; secularization and the rise of science; more autonomy for the individual; a decline in traditions and an increase in rationality, particularly in morals and the law. As differentiation of functions proceeds, the number of rules or norms in society increases, but they relate only to their specialized sphere, and so they carry less weight in society and can more easily allow for innovations. In order for rules to become more general they must become more abstract, and this in turn leaves more space for individual divergences [1], p. 303.

In terms of the development of Durkheim's sociology, this first major work is significant for the fact that it appears to give priority to material causal factors at the morphological level of social life, such as population factors and the struggle for existence resulting from increased population density. But it is clear that, as the argument developed, Durkheim's theoretical interest was in cultural and organizational factors. Whilst insisting that sociology should pay attention to all levels of social phenomena, including the morphological level, Durkheim focused his attention on the level at which beliefs and values became crystallized in the form of institutions, where behaviour is regulated by norms backed by sanctions. It is in this sense that he described sociology as the study of institutions. In *The Division of Labour* the main institution on which attention is focussed is the law; in other works it was to be education, the family, and religion. After the publication of *The Division of Labour,* Durkheim was concerned to defend himself against the charge that he was a "materialist", because he had given causal primacy to material factors. In his defence he made a statement that has since been used to suggest that his sociology became completely idealist. The statement was to the effect that "The principal social phenomena, religion, ethics, law, economy, and aesthetics, are nothing else but a system of values". (Durkheim, 'Jugements de valeurs', in *Sociologie et Philosophie,* [2], p. 140). However, it was the process of institutionalization of values, and the articulation of different levels of social phenomena, that remained the focus of Durkheimian sociology and especially of his theory of social change.

Durkheim's theory of change in *The Division of Labour* has been misinterpreted or underestimated at various times in sociology. Recently there has begun to develop a better appreciation of its innovative basic idea that as societies evolve over time and take on different organizational characteristics, they are subject to different sources of conflict and disruption. It is a mistake to judge the theory as giving priority either to materialist or idealist (cultural) factors; the main focus is on the changing nature of social organization and the consequent changes in the source of conflict. His suggestion is that the potential for conflict increases under two different sets of conditions, each of which is relevant for a society at a given degree of complexity. In the first set of conditions, when a society with low social differentation experiences an increase in population size and density, there is increased competition for scarce resources. Increased differentiation (specialized division of labour) is then one possible resolution to the intensifying struggle for existence. However, such a development raises new problems, for as it frees "itself from the framework which encloses it", it engenders opposition from those supportive of that social framework and structure [1], pp. 183-4. Groups seeking change induce opposition and resistance from those in power who seek to maintain the old "political-familial" order.

The situation in societies which reach a more complex division of labour is different. According to the ideal type, increased differentiation of functions should ease the problems of competition for scarce resources, and produce greater interdependence. However, Durkheim's theory proceeds to enumerate some of the conditions which, in practice, produce conflict. He refers to these as the "forced" and "anomic" forms of the division of labour. The forced division of labour occurs whenever labour is divided in the presence of persisting social inequalities, especially those perpetuated through the hereditary transmisssion of wealth. In such circumstances, conflict in the form of class or civil war will result [1], pp. 374-88.

The anomic division of labour occurs where norms regulating activities break down or fail to emerge. One source of this anomie was where rapid economic change gave rise to new "interests in conflict (which) have not yet had time to be equilibrated" [1], p. 370. Another source was where discrepancies exist between a group's expectations and their achievements. In a such a condition of "relative deprivation", norms governing the means to goal attainment break down, and anomie and increased disorder could result. Some sociologists have sought to make international comparisons, maintaining that, on the basis of this theory, it should be possible to predict that in countries with an advanced division of labour, greater inequality and/or deprivation and/or rapid rate of change would be important predictors of higher levels of political instability and conflict. Empirical studies carried out along these lines, comparing societies in terms of indicators of these variables, tend to give some support to the thesis. (cf Peter G. Sinden [3]).

3.4.8 Crticicisms and developments of Durkheim's ideas in *The Division of Labour*

Some of the criticisms that have been levelled against the theoretical framework and the empirical evidence of *The Division of Labour* have already been mentioned. The theoretical weaknesses are mainly in the evolutionary framework and the organic analogy, and they are defects of which Durkheim himself was in some respects conscious. From time to time he pointed out that this kind of "scaffolding" would have to be dismantled, once the bases of proper causal analysis had been established. He also sought to make clear that he did not believe in a unilinear course of evolution for all societies, but rather thought that comparative sociology should have in mind various abstract models or ideal types along a developmental continuum, and that actual research would use this as a reference point against which to analyse specific deviations in existing societies. The developmental continuum was drawn up in relation to his problematic of issues concerning the relation of the individual to society — issues of forms of organization and social integration. Thus the contrast between the extreme ideal types of mechanical and organic solidarity was not on the same level of comparison as the more historically and economically specific types used by Marx, when discussing capitalism and its immediate predecessor: feudalism. If this is kept in mind, then there is no insuperable barrier or opposition between the theories of Marx and Durkheim; they are potentially complementary, or at least mutually cross-fertilizing.

Unfortunately, Durkheim has been held responsible for many subsequent developments in sociological analysis with which he might not have agreed. The so-called functionalist, or neo-Durkheimian, theory of industrial society and of organizations is an example of guilt by association (or guilt by inspiration), so far as Durkheim is concerned. The charges are that Durkheim neglected the inherent class divisions of capitalism by virtue of his depiction of a single type of industrial society based on an advanced division of labour, and that he regarded the anomic and abnormal forms of the division of labour as exceptional rather than inherent in the capitalist system itself. It is then suggested that subsequent management theories such as those of the Human Relations School, directed towards getting the workers to understand and appreciate their role in the differentiated work process, and to give their commitment to management goals, are in a direct line of succession from Durkheim's arguments about the importance of the moral regulation of industry. However, this interpretation ignores the context in which Durkheim made his remarks about workers' anomie, and it distorts Durkheim's political position by making it seem as if his main concern was with maintaining and promoting capitalism, when in fact his sympathies were with socialism. The fact that socialist societies have still had to wrestle with problems of workers' anomie — that is, with developing forms of work organization and political/economic organization that are meaningful to the individual — shows that Durkheim's problematic had a general relevance. Furthermore, management theories and policies which concentrate on rectifying problems of the anomic division of labour, deriving from the absence of norms to which the worker can feel attached, ignore Durkheim's other pathological condition — the forced division of labour. Durkheim was quite explicit that external inequalities and injustices would have to be removed before there could be a spontaneous division of labour based on freedom. Whereas the problematic of the management theorist gives priority to questions of increasing efficiency, Durkheim's problematic revolved around the issue of reconciling individual freedom and social solidarity.

Within the field of the sociology of industry, Eldridge [4] has shown how the two sources of deviance from the ideal type of spontaneous organic solidarity — the anomic and the forced — can lead to different consequences and require different solutions. In the case of anomie, there are two possible consequences. One general consequence is that the absence of regulation can lead to unspecified desires, and the other is that for the individual specialist worker, work itself can lose its meaning. With regard to the forced division of labour, the possible consequences are, firstly, a resentment of exploitation and an attempt to meet force with force (resistance or revolution); secondly, there is the response of fatalistic acceptance of domination. In a society where anomic and forced division of labour are combined, the unlimited desires/resentment and meaninglessness/fatalism pairs reinforce each other. Some critics (e.g. Horton [5]) have sought to contrast Durkheim's concept of anomie with Marx's concept of alienation, but the contrast only holds up if anomie is kept separate from the forced division of labour; whereas in practice, as Durkheim perceived, they are frequently combined. There can be absence of regulation (anomie) at one level and coercive regulation at another level (forced division of labour), as exemplified by unrestricted competition and lack of agreement over the regulation of prices and incomes, on the one hand, and inequality of opportunities on the other. However, in Durkheim's view, spontaneous attachment to norms (as distinct from coerced attachment deriving from an imposed ideology) could only occur when the forced division of labour was mitigated. As Alan Fox has emphasized, although Durkheim did not believe mitigation of the forced division of labour would in itself cope with the problem of anomie, he did regard it as an essential precondition [6], pp. 234–5. This is ignored by critics who have accused him of inspiring a belief in the capacity of managerial human relations techniques for curing workers' anomie. He made it clear anomie could only be dispelled by policies based on equality and justice. The most important contribution that he made to contemporary studies of work organization, trades unionism and industrial relations, was in insisting on the significance of social justice, ethics and values. (See, for examples, Michael Poole's discussion of Durkheim's influence on members of the 'Oxford School' of industrial relations, such as Alan Fox, Allan Flanders, and Hugh Clegg [7].)

3.4.9   Changes in Durkheim's sociology of law and punishment

In *The Division of Labour,* Durkheim used systems of law and punishment as an indicator of different types of social integration. He drew a sharp contrast between two systems of law: one dominated by repressive sanctions and corresponding to mechanical solidarity, and the other characterized by a predominance of restitutive principles corresponding to organic solidarity. Critics pointed out that the contrast was overdrawn, and also that many of the societies he used as examples of mechanical solidarity and repressive penal systems were in fact not simple tribal or clan societies, but already possessed the rudiments of central state organization, as in the case of the ancient Jewish and Roman societies. However, he made some strategic alterations to his sociology of law and punishment in his article, 'Two Laws of Penal Evolution' [8] first published in *L'Année sociologique* in 1900. This article responded to some of the criticisms by modifying the former opposition between repressive sanctions and restitutive principles.

The most important additions or modifications to his original thesis were concerned with his classification of crimes, and with regard to the political factor. Whereas, in the original thesis, the main contrast was between repressive and restitutive sanctions, in the later article the contrast involves a classification of crimes into those that are fundamentally religious in character — offences against shared moral tenets that constitute the collective conscience — and those that are "individual", in the sense of involving the essentially private interests of increasingly autonomous individuals. Penal sanctions also change in quantity and quality, with a movement away from corporal punishment and toward depriving the individual of possessions or freedom, i.e. fines and imprisonment. This development corresponds to the increasing differentiation within society, and the increasing focus on the individual, in this case as criminal or victim. Durkheim makes an interesting point about prisons only coming into existence when a society reached a sufficiently advanced stage of material development to permit the existence of secure and fortified establishments, such as castles or other large dwellings of a king or class of notables.

With regard to the political factor, Durkheim conceded that the process of differentiation within society, as the key determinant of law and punishment, might be temporarily overshadowed by the effects brought about by variations in political institutions. The specific case he had in mind was where governmental power became absolute, with no countervailing limitation from other institutions. In such situations, punishments would become more severe and repressive. Durkheim regarded such occurences as exceptional deviations from the normal course of development. However, later studies of the pattern of political development, especially of colonial states, tend to suggest that repressive law may be a normal feature at a certain stage of development. Criminalization of offences that were previously treated as purely civil matters seems to occur in the period when a state is being newly formed and wishes to assert its authority over traditional and local institutions previously oriented to restitutive justice. This repressive penal policy may be yet another example of the symbolic functions of punishment, about which Durkheim wrote with such insight. In this case the newly-emerging state institutions seek to assert their hegemony over other institutions and over the minds of the citizens, and so anything that detracts from the dignity and authority of the State is severely punished.

Law and Penal Policy – Modifications and Criticisms

Before examining some of the criticisms that have been levelled against Durkheim's sociology of law, and the modifications and alternatives that have been suggested, it is worth noting that even his most severe critic maintains that "there is also an underlying validity in the importance that Durkheim attaches to the law for any understanding of society" [9], p. 36. Certainly the phenomenon of law was of crucial importance in Durkheim's sociological model because it was an external indicator of a level of social life at which moral forces became crystallized and institutionalized to a degree where they were formalized and backed by sanctions.

The most common criticism is that Durkheim overestimated the extent to which law is repressive in pre-industrial societies, and underestimated the extent to which repressive law continues in industrial societies. An early review of *The Division of Labour*, when it appeared in English in 1933, pointed out that anthropological evidence acquired in the forty years since the book's first appearance showed that there was much division of labour and little repressive law in primitive societies [10]. One of the most famous pieces of anthropological research that seemed to provide evidence contrary to Durkheim's thesis was carried out by Malinowski in the Trobriand Islands [11]. It stressed the reciprocal and tolerant nature of the Trobrianders' social relations and the non-religious basis of their legal system. A later summary of ethnographic evidence by Barnes also came to the conclusion that the evidence did not substantiate Durkheim's claim that society's evolutionary development had been accompained by a change in the law from repressive to restitutive. Barnes maintained that "the ethnographic evidence shows that, in general, primitive societies are not characterized by repressive laws", and that "it is governmental action that is typically repressive" [12], pp. 168-9.

A more radical criticism is to the effect that Durkheim was right in positing a parallel development in the division of labour and in legal systems, but that he got it the wrong way round. Sheleff maintains that the development has been in the direction of more repressive law. In his view the repressive nature of modern legal systems may be a consequence of the degree of homogeneity and conformity which mass society has imposed on modern man, as noted by sociologists of different political persuasions, from the conservative Ortega y Gasset to the radical C. Wright Mills, from Riseman's other-directed man to Marcuse's one-dimensional man. The criminalization of offences against moral standards and government regulations has been examined from various angles, ranging from sociologists concerned with social reform (who may advocate the use of the law to control pollution or enforce the wearing of seat-belts in cars), to sociologists of deviance who criticize those "moral entrepreneurs" who try to use the criminal law to have their standards of morality imposed on all of the population (cf Howard Becker [13]). Two prominent approaches to the sociology of deviance — conflict and labelling — have pointed to the repressive aspects of modern legal systems, and have focused attention on the political process by which acts become defined as criminal, and on the practical administrative process of police, judicial, and correctional actions by which an individual becomes defined as deviant. Both these theories stress the social need for stigmatizing deviant groups and deviant acts, and draw some inspiration from Durkheim's own analysis of the functional importance for society of finding an outlet for its hostility against deviant groups as a means of contributing to the solidarity of the community.

An important factor modifying Durkheim's original thesis is that of the political structure. Durkheim placed his emphasis on the general process of increasing division of labour and structural differentiation within modern society. However, the emergence and growth of the State as the dominant institution, or institutional complex, has presented a major deviation from Durkheim's postulated trend. Although he tried to take account of the political factor in his later article, "Two Laws of Penal Development", he still regarded the increase of repressive law as a temporary deviation brought about by the pathological form of "absolute" State. He limited his analysis of governmental authoritarianism to its impact on the intensity and type of punishment, without going on to consider its possible impact on social structure and the nature of law. If, as seems likely, it is a normal occurrence for governments of industrial societies to use penal sanctions to maintain control over wide areas of social life, it would be necessary to modify Durkheim's thesis that the normal course of development is for repressive law to diminish as the division of labour increases. A compromise position, suggested by some sociologists, modifies Durkheim's thesis of a unilinear development of the law and puts forward a curvilinear sequence (Du Bow [14]). According to this view, there is a move from restitutive law in the most simple societies, to repressive law in the early stages of the establishment of a State as it attempts to gain a monopoly of the legitimate use of coercion, followed by a return to restitutive law when the State has become established and mature. Civil and restitutive law can predominate when there is a high degree of social solidarity and value integration, and criminal law predominates when the emerging State has still to establish its ideological hegemony. This curvilinear development thesis still entails a modification of Durkheim's view that simple societies needed repressive law in order to maintain social solidarity. However, it does not go against most of the empirical evidence cited by Durkheim, because the majority of the cases he cited as examples of non-industrial societies with a high degree of repressive law were in fact at the stage of developing a central state organization.

REFERENCES

[1] Emile Durkhiem, *The Division of Labour in Society,* trs. George Simpson, New York, Free Press paperback edn, 1964.

[2] Emile Durkheim, *Sociologie et Philosophie,* Paris, Presses Universaires de France, 1951.

[3] Peter G. Sinden, "Political Instability, Durkheim and the Division of Labour: A Cross-National Analysis", *Humboldt Journal of Social Relations,* 6, 2, 1979, pp. 46–78.

[4] John Eldridge, *Sociology and Industrial Life,* London, Michael Joseph, 1971.

[5] John Horton, "The Dehumanisation of Anomie and Alienation: A Problem in the Ideology of Sociology", *British Journal of Sociology,* vol. 15, no. 4, pp. 283-300.

[6] Alan Fox, *Beyond Contract: Work, Power and Trust Relations,* London, Faber, 1974.

[7] Michael Poole, *Theories of trade unionism: A sociology of industrial relations,* London, Routledge and Kegan Paul, 1981.

[8] Emile Durkheim, "Two Laws of Penal Evolution" in Mark Traugott (ed.), *Emile Durkheim on Institutional Analysis,* Chicago, University of Chicago Press, 1978.

[9] Leon, S. Sheleff, "From Restitutive Law to Repressive Law: Durkheim's *The Division of Labour in Society* revisited" *European Journal of Sociology,* **XVI**, 1, 1975, pp. 16-45.

[10] E. Faris, Book review in *American Journal of Sociology,* **XL**, 1934, p. 367.

[11] B. Malinowski, *Argonauts of the Western Pacific,* New York, Dutton, 1922.

[12] John Barnes, "Durkheim's *Division of Labour in Society",* *Man,* n.s. **1**, 1966, pp. 158-75.

[13] Howard, Becker, *Outsider: Studies in the sociology of deviance,* New York, Free Press, 1963.

[14] Fred Du Bow, "Nation-Building and the Imposition of Criminal Law", paper delivered to the American Sociological Association Annual Meeting, August 1974, in Montreal Canada.

3.5 THE RULES OF SOCIOLOGICAL METHOD

3.5.1 Character of the book — manifesto and transitional

The *Rules* [1] is a manifesto for the cause of scientific sociological analysis. It is not a distillation of lessons learned in doing sociological research. The strength of his advocacy of certain methodological positions arose from his polemical interest in asserting the claims of sociology against contemporary detractors or rivals, and in distancing himself from unscientific predecessors. It has even been suggested that methodological interests were not dominant in his thinking, and that he regarded methods in a purely instrumental manner, so much so that he would have agreed with the remark of another social scientist that "discussing methodology is like playing the slide trombone. It has to be done extraordinarily well if it is not to be more interesting to the person who does it than to others who listen to it" [2]. However, he was a devasting critic of inadequate methods, as can be seen in his reviews in the *Année*.

Because of its manifesto-like character, it would be unfair to judge Durkheim's methodological position on the basis of the *Rules* taken in isolation, just as it would be unfair to judge Marx's methodology and epistemology on the basis of the *Communist Manifesto*. In the case of Marx, a full appreciation of the richness and variety of his methods can only be gained by comparing works as diverse as *Capital,* the *Eighteenth Brumaire of Louis Napoleon,* and others. It is even more important in appreciating Durkheim's position to take account of the full range of his works, from the early reviews, where he can be seen working out his own position in relation to his predecessors and contemporaries (especially the German social scientists), through to his later works on primitive classification and religion, and including neglected but important works such as *The Evolution of Educational Thought* [3].

An examination of some of these works makes it plain that his methodological ideals in the *Rules* only partly resembled his actual methods. He employed a dialectical form of argument in discussing methods, which entailed setting forth antithetical views that he then criticized and seemingly discarded. But then he would often reincorporate elements of these positions in his own synthesis. This dialectial procedure, whereby he synthesized and reintegrated in his own approach positions which he had first criticized, is more important for understanding his thought than the other procedure he used, which was "argument by elimination", in which alternative positions are systematically rejected in a way meant to lend authority to the sole remaining position — his own. Such an argument proves nothing, as there is no way of knowing whether all the possible alternatives have been considered, nor need the various positions be mutually exclusive.

The *Rules* marked a transitional point in Durkheim's intellectual development. In the *Division of Labour* he had developed and applied his formulation of the subject-matter of sociology — the nature of social solidarity. He had discussed a range of empirical phenomena, including changes in the social sub-structure and corresponding changes in institutions and the collective conscience. He had developed the basis of his method: treating *social facts* as real *things;* asking questions about the sorts of social facts that might have *caused* other social facts to develop in a particular direction; and also asking what was the social need (*function*) served by a social fact such as an institution; and he had tried to develop models or types of sets of social facts that seemed to *normally* fit together (or vary together — *concomitant variation*) at certain points on a continuum; the continuum had been constructed on the basis of a modified *evolutionary* conception, using the developmental analogy of a tree, with a main trunk and branches going off in different directions (thus modifying the unilinear view of evolution).

What had not been fully developed was a conception of collective representations (ideas, concepts, values, and beliefs, etc.) as a crucial and relatively independent set of explanatory variables. This only emerged after he had written the *Rules* and as a result of acquiring more comparative data, particularly ethnographic data on the potency and variety of collective representations of a religious nature in primitive societies. It also emerged as a result of his growing appreciation of the relative autonomy of institutions once they had evolved beyond the originating phase where they corresponded more closely to the substructure. Before the mature work, in the *Division of Labour* and the *Rules* he was still at the stage of employing a "generic" materialism, which has been broadly defined as an explanatory framework wherein the more concrete and "objective" elements are seen as causes of those which are more abstract and conceptual.

In the *Rules*, despite his firmness in asserting correct procedures for sociological analysis, and his polemical rejection of all explanations which ignored the specificity of the social element in social phenomena, the work is not decisive in identifying which explanatory variables should be given priority with regard to specific topics. At one point he says that morphological facts "play a preponderant role in collective life, and hence in sociological explanations"[1], p. 112. But he goes on to say that in these "morphological" elements, which constitute the internal environment of a social group (just as an anatomy of an organism constitutes its internal milieu), should be sought "the first origins of all social processes of any importance"[1], p. 113. He is being more specific here in suggesting that morphological (substructural) factors are preponderant in originating an institution, but it is not clear how they continue determining its present shape and functioning. Indeed, he rejected the idea that historical study of past events and states could provide a sufficient explanation of present conditions:

"If . . . all the principal causes of social events were in the past, each society would no longer be anything but the prolongation of its predecessor, and the different societies would lose their individuality and would become only diverse moments of one and the same evolution"[1], p. 120.

The clue as to how morphological factors could continue to play a determining role is contained in his use of the biological analogy of the internal milieu of an organism. At this stage of his intellectual development he did not go further than to suggest that it was the particular structural arrangement of the society that constituted the internal environment of its psychic life and activity. The only energizing or transforming force that he mentioned to link the structure to consciousness and activity, was that generated by increased dynamic density of social exchanges with growth in the division of labour. This all sounds very mechanical. He might have improved it by making a more explicit use of the concept of the internal milieu as it had been developed by the famous French biologist, Claude Bernard, a contemporary whose work he admired. Bernard's physiology had united the analysis of the cellular level and the study of more complex organic functions by distinguishing between the *milieu extérieur* in which the organism is situated, and a *milieu intérieur* in which the tissue elements lived. The living organism did not really exist in the *milieu extérieur* (the atmosphere it breathes, salt or fresh water if that was its element) but in the liquid *milieu intérieur* formed by the circulating organic liquid which surrounds and bathes all the tissue elements, i.e. lymph or plasma. It was this internal milieu that mediated between the environment and the life of the organism. Durkheim's later work, especially that on collective representations, education, and socialization, suggested ways in which the social environment was internalized by the individual in socialization. But even at the stage of writing the *Rules* ne had begun to insist that there was no gap between material and cultural structures.

He had broadened the sense of morphology to include underlying structures that were a fusion of material *and* mental factors. Thus, the territorial structure of a society was itself constituted by mental phenomena such as laws:

> "Indeed, when we wish to know how a society is divided politically, of what these divisions themselves are composed, and how complete is the fusion existing between them, we shall not achieve our purposes by physical inspection and by geographical observations; for these phenomena are social, even when they have some basis in physical nature. It is only by a study of public law that a comprehension of this organization is possible, for it is this law that determining the organization, as it equally determines our domestic and civil relations"[1], p. 11.

Between the various levels of social phenomena, from the substructure to the most fluid currents of social life, there were only differences in degree of consolidation or crystallization. The analogy with an organism appears to break down in the social sphere, because it is difficult to separate out, or draw a line, between anatomy and physiology, the fixed and the fluid. As he admits in a footnote:

> "This close connection between life and structure, organ and function, may be easily proved in sociology because between these two extreme terms there exists a whole series of immediately observable intermediate stages which show the bond between them. Biology is not in the same favourable position. But we may well believe that the inductions on this subject made by sociology are applicable to biology and that, in organisms as well as in societies, only differences in degree exist between these two orders of facts"[1], p. 13.

The study of genetic codes such as DNA in biology, since Durkheim's time, has made his use of the organic analogy seem more plausible than it once did. It is now possible to see how the fixed and the fluid, structure and process (processes of thinking and acting in society), can be fused into one. The various layers of the social organism, like the internal milieu of a biological organism, are governed by certain basic codes. It is in this way that the internal milieu of the society is also internalized by the individual. Thanks to these codes, especially symbolic codes, there is a correspondence between the organization of society and its collective representations, and these are reflected in the consciousness of the individual. In this way society continually reproduces itself. It is this social reproduction, based on the integration (solidarity) of individual and society, that constitutes the subject-matter of Durkheim's sociology. However, when writing the *Rules* he had not yet carried out his detailed investigations of the correspondence between substructures and symbolic codes, which formed the topic of his later work on primitive classification and the elementary forms of religion.

In the *Rules* we find him struggling to synthesize two different traditions, partly national traditions (German and British), of nineteenth-century social thought. German *Volkerpsychologie* had stressed the intellectual, emotional, and volitional unity of social groups. But along with this, Durkheim emphasized the structural characteristics of social integration advanced by Spencer, who used the organic analogy to describe the interrelationship of specialized parts of a total structure. From Durkheim's fusion of these two traditions came his characteristic statement that collective beliefs and norms grow around sustained patterns of social interaction. Unfortunately, the fusion was not adequately theorized, and Durkheim has been criticized by Gouldner, among others, for failing to distinguish between "patterns of social interaction, or social structures, and (cultural) patterns of moral beliefs or sentiments"[4], p. 25.

The result is that commentators have attached quite contradictory labels to his position, depending on which of the two traditions or notions of structure they consider to have been dominant in his thought. In his own time, when his reputation was beginning to be established on the basis of the *Division of Labour* and the *Rules,* he was thought to adhere to a materialist-organicist view. According to this view, morphology refers to the concrete structure or pattern of groups and sub-groups, the order or arrangement of which gives the society its characteristic physiognomy. In the preface to the second edition of the *Rules* Durkheim hastened to deny that, because he had said social facts should be regarded as things, he was therefore stating that social facts were ultimately nothing but material things. He denied that he held to this kind of "realism". He claimed that, far from "eliminating the mental element from sociology" he had "expressly stated and reiterated that social life is constituted wholly of collective 'representations' "[1], p. xli. This has since led some critics to label him as an "idealist" − one who sees society as an interdependent set of beliefs and ideas. And it is certainly the case that his later work gave prominence to the cultural phenomena, such as linguistic symbols, religious beliefs, and moral norms. But despite the varying emphases that he gave to the two sets of factors in his different works, there is no doubt that he was searching for a way of disclosing the principles of correspondence by which certain patterns of social interaction and patterns of beliefs and ideas could be shown to have an affinity for each other. The discovery of these principles would require the classification of social types in terms of the mode of combination of their component elements. In the *Rules* the discussion of the method of classification is mainly taken up with examples of types of social organization, from the most simple unit, the "horde", throught the segmental type called a "clan", to more complex combinations. In his later work he was to devote more attention to classifications of a cultural sort and their correspondence with the types of social organization, mainly in simple societies, as in the case of totemic beliefs in societies with clan-based organization.

3.5.2 Classification of social types
The purpose in drawing up classifications of social types was to make it possible to test hypotheses about the reltionships between social phenomena. The classification of types of social organization (or

species) would facilitate this scientific endeavour because it would make it unnecessary to examine every separate case before making a generalization. A classification based on a few essential principles would yield a typology that the sociologist could use when making comparisons (the nearest thing to an experimental method in sociology), so that he or she would not have to observe every society of this type before being able to establish a generalization:

> "Once the classification is established on this principle, in order to know whether a fact is general throughout a species it will be unnecessary to observe all societies of this species; a few will suffice. Even one well-made observation will be enough in many cases, just as one well-constructed experiment often suffices for the establishment of a law"[1], p. 80.

Sociology would then be able to work at an intermediate level between that of the ethnographers and historians, who examined single societies, and at the other extreme, the social philosophers and early sociologists like Comte and Spencer, who made sweeping generalizations about mankind as though it constituted one great Society.

The principles of classification in their full range would only be discovered when sociology had developed its explanatory powers to a sufficient degree, but at the stage of writing the *Rules*, Durkheim said, enough was known to conjecture that the principles should be found in modes of combination:

> "We know that societies are composed of various parts in combination. Since the nature of the aggregate depends necessarily on the nature and number of the component elements and their mode of combination, these characteristics are evidently what we must take as our basis; and we shall see from what follows that it is on them that the general facts of social life depend. Moreover, as they are of the morphological order, one could call the part of sociology which has for its task the constitution and classification of social types, 'social morphology' "[1], pp. 81-82.

Durkheim criticized Spencer for not defining precisely in theoretical terms what he meant by a simple society when he classified societies in evolutionary stages, from simple to complex. According to Durkheim, Spencer's view seemed to equate simplicity with crudity of organization. On this basis the most dissimilar societies would be grouped together: ". . . the Homeric Greeks are placed parallel with the holders of feudal estates in the tenth century, and below the Bechauanas, the Zulus, and the Fijians; the Athenian confederation is parallel to the feudal estates of thirteen-century France, and below the Iroquois and the Araucanians"[1], p. 82. Durkheim defined "simplicity" as complete absence of parts, meaning in the social realm a single segment with no trace of previous segmentation, which he called a "horde". The horde was thus "the protoplasm of the social realm, and consequently, the natural basis of classification" [1], p. 83. It was directly composed of individuals, in "atomic juxtaposition". It did not matter whether such hordes had ever existed — they were logically required in order to provide the simplest social unit in his theoretical classification of social types. More complex types could then be distinguished within the classification, such as "simple polysegmental socities", e.g. certain Iroquois and Australian tribes. There were also combinations of poly-segmental societies, such as the "polysegmental societies simply com-pounded", e.g. the Iroquois Confederation;and "polysegmental societies doubly compounded", e.g. the Roman city-state, an aggregate of tribes, which are themselves aggregates of *curiae,* which in turn resolve them-sevles into clans. [1], p. 84.

Durkheim suggested that this classification would become more complex as new combinations were discovered, based on secondary characteristics. However, in the second edition of the book he added a footnote to the chapter on classification of social types. In this he said that he had not mentioned the method of classification of species according to their state of civilization because none had been proposed by "authoritative sociologists. . .save perhaps the too evidently archaic one of Comte"[1], p. 88, footnote 10. Since that time several attempts in this direction had been made, but Durkheim said he would not discuss them because they referred to the classification of historical phases rather than social species. To adopt such classifications would make it possible for a society to seem to have changed its characteristics several times:

> "Since its origin, France has passed through very different forms of civilization; it began by being agricultural, passed to craft industry and to small commerce then to manufacturing, and finally to large-scale industry. Now it is impossible to admit that the same collective individuality can change its species three or four times. A species must define itself by more constant characteristics"[1], p. 88.

Durkheim wanted to confine the principle of classification to something more deeply embedded and durable than civilizational characteristics such as economic and technical organization, or artistic and scientific culture:

> "The economic state, technological state, etc., present phenomena too unstable and complex to furnish the basis of a classification. It is even very proable that the same industrial, scientific, and artistic civilization can be found in societies whose *hereditary constitution* is very different. Japan may in the future borrow our arts, our industry, even our political organization; it will not cease to belong to a different social species from France and Germany"[1], p. 88, emphasis added.

Unfortunately, he laid himself open to the criticism that he had pressed the biological analogy too far in that, whilst individual animals cannot change their species, because the species' characteristics are part of the animal itself, it does not follow that an individual society cannot change its social species without ceasing to exist as that society. In Durkheim's view, feudal France was the same social species as the France of his own Third Republic and what changes there had been were merely secondary matters of "civilization". For the purpose of analysing developments in complex societies, Marx's classification in terms of a "civilizational" aspect, mode of economic production, has proved much more useful, whereas Durkheim's classification of societal types has been used more extensively by social anthropologists studying simpler societies. However, Durkheim's reference to the different *hereditary constitutions* of societies could have some relevance to the study of complex societies. In part it echoes a theme in the work of the German historians who had influenced Durkheim's early intellectual development — the stress on societies as "cultural entities" that outlasted changes in civilizational aspects, such as mode of production. But Durkheim was not referring to cultural entities like the "race" or the "national spirit", as some conservative Germans were when they wrote about *Kultur* being more fundamental than civilizational factors. The "herediatry constitution" was more likely a reference to the type of combination of structure that had created a society. The only doubt is whether the types of combination could be limited to a manageable number in drawing up a classification of social species of modern societies. He did not say how Japan, Germany, and France differed in this respect. If each country had a unique combination of structures in its "hereditary constitution", then each society was a separate social species, and Durkheim's claims for the scientific value of his classification would have to be rejected. It is unlikely that he would have wished to insist that each society was a separate social species, but he did not return to the task of developing his classification of societal types, and so we cannot say how he would have distinguished complex societies in terms of secondary structural characteristics.

3.5.3 Rules of observation and explanation of social facts

Social Facts as Things

We have already come across some of Durkheim's main rules for sociological observation, most notably in his statement that, "The first and most fundamental rule is: Consider social facts as things" [1], p. 14. To which he added, "To treat phenomena as things is to treat them as data, and these constitute the point of departure of science" [1], p. 27. By advocating treating them as things, he meant we should adopt a certain attitude toward them of mature scepticism with regard to common assumptions and preconceptions. The phenomena could only be explained scientifically through the study of their externally observable characteristics or indications: "They cannot be perceived or known directly, but only through the phenomenal reality expressing them" [1] , p. 27. Even phenomena which seem purely arbitrary, or the result of someone's will, on further investigation reveal qualities of consistency or regularity which are symptomatic of their objectivity. Nor can such facts be altered very easily by a mere act of the will; they are recalcitrant and require strenuous effort if they are to be changed. "Far from being a product of the will, they determine it from without; they are like moulds in which our actions are inevitably shaped" [1] , p. 29.

Durkheim has been criticized for these statements. One criticism is that he seemed to think that the proof of the existence of an objective fact was that it was resistant to change, in the same way as matter resists modification. The second criticism is that this gave his sociology an inherently conservative bias because it made it seem as if the natural state of social phenomena was static and that there were no intrinsic forces making for dynamic change. However, what he really had in mind was the difficulty of changing institutions in an arbitrary fashion, without regard for the causal network in which they were embedded. He was particularly opposed to humanist doctrines which taught that human nature had a specific and circumscribed character, which was expressed in institutions. Human nature and ideas about it were extremely variable, and they varied according to the social situation, said Durkheim. Humanist doctrines could give rise to both conservative and revolutionary excesses, because they were not based on sociological structuralist analysis. This was to be Durkheim's conclusion after surveying the history of educational ideologies in different periods:

"To sum up, human nature as it manifests itself in history is above all something which we can and should credit with amazing flexibility and fecundity. We need not fear that this conviction will cause men's minds to swing abruptly from neophobia, which is one kind of evil, to what is a different but no lesser evil, namely revolutionary excess. What history teaches us is that man does not change arbitrarily; he does not transform himself at will on hearing the voices of inspired prophets. The reason is that all change, in colliding with the inherited institutions of the past, is inevitably hard and laborious; consequently it only takes place in response to the demands of necessity. For change to be brought about it is not enough that it should be seen as desirable; it must be the product of changes within the whole network of diverse causal relationships which determine the situation of man"[3], pp. 329-30.

Ideological Analysis

In *The Evolution of Educational Thought* [3] Durkheim was concerned with showing the relationship between systems of ideas (educational doctrines) and the specific social needs of the time, especially the functions they served for particular classes or strata. This constituted a sociological analysis of ideology (something which a number of critics, usually Marxists, have claimed not to be able to find in Durkhiem's works). However, he also wrote in the *Rules* using the term "ideology" to refer to the much broader topic of the preconceptions and ideas that people have about things. What he criticized as "ideological analysis" was the tendency to substitute for the study of things, the study of popular preconceptions and ideas about those things, thus mistaking the idea for the thing itself. Scientific sociology must go behind people's preconceptions and, using external indicators as clues, disclose the underlying structured reality. Thus, the first negative rule of sociological methodology was that, "All preconceptions must be eradicated"[1], p. 31. But this negative rule only "teaches the sociologist to escape the realm of lay ideas and to turn his attention toward facts, but it does not tell him how to take hold of the facts in order to study them objectively"[1], p. 34.

Definition of Concepts

A second rule was necessary: "The subject matter of every sociological study should comprise a group of phenomena defined in advance by certain external characteristics, and all phenomena so defined should be included within this group."[1], p. 35. His favourite example was crime:

> "For example, we note the existence of certain acts, all presenting the external characteristic that they evoke from society the particular reaction called punishment. We constitute them as a separate group, to which we give a common label; we call every punished act a crime, and crime thus defined becomes the object of a special science, criminology"[1], p. 35-6.

New concepts often had to be formulated appropriate to the requirements of science, but lay concepts were not entirely useless to the scholar: "they serve as suggestions and guides. They inform us of the existence, somewhere, of an aggregation of phenomena which, bearing the same name, must in consequence probably have certain characteristics in common."[1], p. 37. Failure to define the object of study, Durkheim suggested, was perhaps the most common error in sociology: "Precisely because sociology treats everyday things, such as the family, property, crime, etc., the sociologist most often thinks it unnecessary to define them rigorously at the outset."[1], p. 37.

Normal and Abnormal

The next rule presented by Durkheim was for distinguishing between the normal and the abnormal: "A social fact is normal, in relation to a given social type at a given phase of its development, when it is present in the average society of that species at the corresponding phase of its evolution."[1], p. 64. He hoped that by establishing which phenomena normally appeared together, and their normal rates of frequency or strength, it would be possible to give factual grounds for judging something to be deviant, or pathological. For example, instead of judging all crime to be deviant or pathological, which might simply be a judgement based on personal bias, the sociologist would be aware that crime was present in all societies as a normal phenomenon (possibly serving some positive functions). Sociological comparative analysis would show that it was the types and rates of crime that varied, some of which were normal for a particular type of society and others abnormal.

According to Durkheim, classification of social facts as normal or abnormal in relation to social types and species is part of the lead-in to the main task of sociology, which is that of explanation.

Summary of Rules of Explanation

The main rules for the explanation of social facts can be summarized as follows [1] :

(1) "When, then, the explanation of a social phenomenon is undertaken, we must seek separately the efficient cause which produces it and the function it fulfils." p. 95.
(2) "The determining cause of a social fact should be sought among the social facts preceding it and not among the states of the individual consciousness." p. 110.
(3) "The function of a social fact ought always to be sought in its relation to some social end." p. 111.
(4) "The first origins of all social processes of any importance should be sought in the internal constitution of the social group." p. 113.

Causal Explanation

In Durkheim's view, causal analysis was essential to sociology if it was to be a science. Because of the complexity of sociological data it might not always be possible to establish a simple cause and effect relation, but the sociologist could unravel an intricate causational situation. Unfortunately, Durkheim sometimes gave his causal theories a mechanistic tone, so as to strengthen his case for the scientific status of sociology. An example of this is to be found in the way in which he argued his case in the *Division of Labour,* which scandalized the examiners when it was submitted for a doctoral degree. However, the explanation was not as mechanical as Durkheim made it sound. At first reading it might seem as if the division of labour was directly caused by an increase in population denisty; but, as we have seen, the causal links were more complex, and included an increase in moral or dynamic density (social interaction). This moral density could also be broken down into a set of social factors — number and frequency of social contracts, number of qualitatively different types of social relations, and the degree of intimacy of the social relationships.

Causal explanation did not stop with establishing that factors varied together and therefore might be causally related. The causal connection had to be made intelligible, which entailed asking why an increase in social interaction necessitated a growth in the division of labour. The intermediary links had to be spelled out in terms of the ideational factors — the values held in society, which made it likely that people would respond to the increased struggle for existence by engaging in greater specialization of functions (division of labour) rather than by emigrating, commiting suicide, resorting to civil war or crime. Durkheim also added to these causal factors another set of factors that he referred to as necessary conditions, permissive factors, or secondary factors. They were factors that made a development possible but did not directly cause it. In the example of the division of labour they included the greater independence of individuals relative to the group, and also the existence of conducive organico-psychical bases of individual behaviour. The first type of factor accounted for the space or slack in the relation of the individual to the group, which allowed for individual variation to occur. The second factor made the variations biologically and psychologically possible.

Functionalism

Durkheim's methodological rules specified that causal explanation should be supplemented by functional explanation. While the social usefulness of a phenomenon did not explain how it had come into being, because it was often impossible to verify the kind of explanation that said something had come into being because it was deliberately willed with a view to satisfying certain ends, social utility could make intelligible some of the intervening links that might explain why the phenomenon persists. He used the organic analogy to make intelligible the correspondence between the functions of the instution of Government (the State) and certain needs of modern industrial society, likening it to the brain's functions in relation to the needs of the body. The advantage of the word "function" was that it did not necessarily imply that the correspondence was intentional or deliberate.

Despite his constant references to the functions of social phenomena, Durkheim was well aware of the limitations of the organic analogy. Consequently, he did not develop an elaborate functional model of society, as did some sociologists who were influenced by evolutionary biological theory. He was too aware of the *sui generis* character of the social. One reason for using the concept of function was that it could be used polemically to combat the contemporary tendency to psychological reductionism and the explanation of social institutions in terms of individuals' intentions, as in the Utilitarian assumption that institutions were the product of the individual's search for increased happiness. Durkheim's conception of functionalism was highly flexible. He used it to refer to the *latent* (unintended) functions of institutions, which escaped human notice or intention. He also recognized that institutions could serve multiple functions and that there were functional alternatives; the same institution could serve different functions, and these functions could vary from society to society. With the development of the division of labour the tie between a given function and a given structure could become looser and more flexible — the function becoming increasingly independent of the structure.

Comparative-Historical Approach

In order to disclose these various causal and functional relationships sociology needed to adopt a comparative-historical approach. Because sociology could not carry out experiments it had to rely on the method of indirect experiment — the comparision of similar cases. If two or more phenomena appeared to vary together — concomitant variation or correlation — then it was likely that a causal relationship existed. This would have to be checked against the data, as it was quite possible for two phenomena to vary together because of the action of a third factor:

> "For example, we can establish in the most certain way that the tendency to suicide varies directly with education. But it is impossible to understand how erudition can lead to suicide; such an explanation is in contradiction to the laws of psychology ... Thus we come to ask if both facts are not the consequence of an identical condition. This common cause is the weakening of religious traditionalism, which reinforces both the need for knowledge and the tendency toward suicide"[1], p. 132.

However, comparison must be systematic — it would not do simply to illustrate the hypothesis with a few scattered cases of co-variation. "It is necessary to compare not isolated variations but a series of systematically arranged variations of wide range, in which the individual items tie up with one another in as continuous a gradation as possible."[1], p. 135-6. The way in which the series was formed would depend on whether the comparisons were within a society (e.g. between different groups or areas), between societies of the same social type, or between different types of societies. It was possible to establish concomitant variation within a society with regard to a particular social current, e.g. a suicidogenic current, but when it was an institutions's function that was in question, then it would be necessary to compare different societies or the same society at different times. The most complex social phenomena — social institutions — could only be explained after the most extensive historical and cross-cultural comparisions had been carried out: "Consequently, one cannot explain a social fact of any complexity except by following its complete development through all social species."[1], p. 139. For Durkheim, the comparative-historical approach was the core of sociological methodology. All his researches, and most of those carried out by his colleagues on the *Année* team, were set in a historical framework. It is ironical that the structural-functionalism with which his name came to be associated, after the Second World War, was almost completely ahistorical and incapable of dealing with social change.

3.5.4 Conclusions

The manifesto-like character of the *Rules* renders it unsuitable as a basis for evaluating his actual methods of sociological analysis. These methods are best appreciated in the context of his substantive studies, where their flexibility and variety are evident. This is not to say that he completely ignored his own rules, which were sufficiently general and basic to allow the widest scope in practice. He *did* treat social facts as real things, and search for causes in other social facts; there *are* many references to the social functions of pehnomena, and constructed classifications of social types, within a comparative-historical (sometimes "evolutionary") framework. However, there are many differences in his approaches to specific topics. This should be evident from our review of his main works and the discussion of relevant criticisms in each case. It should also become clear that some of the more sweeping criticisms of his methods are not fully justified; such as the suggestion that his functionalist approach was inevitably conservative and could not explain social change deriving from conflicts inherent in the system. He chose to approach the question of conflict from the direction of viewing social wholes as systems "of forces limiting and containing each other and making an equilibrium."[5], p. 233. But the conception was a dynamic one of constantly changing balances between opposed forces. Realities only existed to the extent that they embodied a force, and forces did not exist in a vacuum but were typically opposed by other forces. The central dynamic was provided by the opposition between the non-social (unsocialized) component of the individual and the integrating forces of society. Contemporary capitalist society was marked by disequilibrium because the socially integrating forces could not match the egoistic forces; economic conflicts were a manifestation of this failure.

The language and analogies used by Durkheim in the *Rules* now appear somewhat dated and inadequate to express formulations of scientific methodology and epistemology. In particular, the biological-organicist analogy had many limitations, both by reason of the intrinsic difference between biological and social phenomena (of which Durkheim was aware), and because of the deficiencies of biological science in his day. However, Durkheim did try to incorporate some of the best ideas of contemporary biology in his methodology, and it is not the case that he ignored the work of the leading French biologist, Claude Bernard (contrary to the suggestion in Hirst [6]). He referred with approval to Bernard's views on scientific methodology. (cf. Traugott, [7], pp. 111 and 209, Parsons [8, 9]). While it may be true that Durkheim did not succeed completely in his attempt to transcend the limitations of existing alternative epistemologies, most critics admit that it was a significant and brave attempt. Like those of Marx and Freud, Durkheim's explanations of behaviour were a scandal in the eyes of many because they contradicted common assumptions, and located causes in deeper structures below the surface level of those phenomena about which we are consciously aware. As Durkheim himself put it in likening his approach to that of Marx:

"We think it a fertile idea that social life must be explained, not by the conception of it created by those who participate in it, but by profound causes which escape awareness..." (quoted in Traugott, [7], p.127.

REFERENCES

[1] Emile Durkheim, *The Rules of Sociological Method*, trs. S. A. Solovay and J. H. Mueller, Chicago, University of Chicago Press, 1938.

[2] Harry Alpert, "Emile Durkheim: A Perspective and Appreciation", in *American Sociological Review*, 24, 4, 1959, p. 462-5.

[3] Emile Durkheim, *The Evolution of Educational Thought*, trs. Peter Collins, London, Routledge and Kegan Paul, 1977.

[4] Alvin W. Gouldner, Introduction to Emile Durkheim, *Socialism*, trs. Charlotte Sattler, New York, Collier Books paperback edn. pp. 7-31.

[5] Emile Durkheim, *The Elementary Forms of the Religious Life*, trs. J. W. Swain, New York, Free Press paperback edn., 1965.

[6] Paul Q. Hirst, *Durkheim, Bernard and Epistemology*, London, Routledge and Kegan Paul, 1975.

[7] Mark Traugott (ed.), *Emile Durkheim on Institutional Analysis*, Chicago, University of Chicago Press, 1978.

[8] Talcott Parsons, "Durkheim on Religion Revisited", in Charles, Y. Glock and Phillip E. Hammond (eds.), *Beyond the Classics? Essays in the Scientific Study of Religion*, New York, Harper and Row, 1973, pp. 156-180.

[9] Talcott Parsons, "Comment on 'Parsons' Interpretation of Durkheim' and on 'Moral Freedom Through Understanding in Durkheim", in *American Sociological Review*, 40, 1, 1975, pp. 106-111.

3.6 SUICIDE

3.6.1 Character and content of the argument

If the *Rules* was a revolutionary manifesto for establishing scientific sociological explanation, it was given its most forceful demonstration in the famous work that followed — *Suicide,* pointedly sub-titled, *A Study in Sociology.* In it he made it quite clear that he was prepared to flout commonsense and excite the kind of incredulity that he believed always greeted science whenever it revealed hidden causes, in this case social forces that were as real as physical forces:

> "Collective tendencies have an existence of their own; they are forces as real as cosmic forces, though of another sort; they, likewise, affect the individual from without, though through other channels. The proof that the reality of collective tendencies is no less than that of cosmic forces is that this reality is demonstrated in the same way, by the uniformity of effects. . . So truly are they things *sui generis* and not mere verbal entities that they may be measured, their relative sizes compared, as is done with the intensity of electric currents or luminous foci. Thus, the basic proposition that social facts are objective, a proposition we have had the opportunity to prove in another work [the *Rules*] and which we consider the fundamental principle of the sociological method, finds a new and especially conclusive proof in moral statistics and above all in the statistic of suicide. Of course it offends common sense. But science has encountered incredulity whenever it has revealed to men the existence of a force that has been overlooked"[1], p. 309-310.

He wanted to demonstrate and establish sociology's scientific status by providing a sociological explanation of that seemingly most individual of acts — suicide. In order to do this he had to define suicide as a social fact that would require explanation in terms of other social facts (social structures and forces as conceptualized in his multi-layered model). The social fact to be explained was not the individual act of suicide, which might be better accounted for by a case study method where, in favourable instances, there might be enough evidence to make inferences about the victim's mental state — motives and intentions. It was suicide *rates,* as disclosed by statistics, that constituted the social fact to be explained as an effect of an imbalance of social structural forces. Consequently, he proceeded to define suicide with the least possible reference to mental elements, excluding any reference to intentions but allowing for the need to distinguish between accidental death and suicide: "the term suicide is applied to all cases of death resulting directly or indirectly from a positive or negative act of the victim himself, which he knows will produce this result."[1], p. 44.

Comparative statistics for countries and categories of people within each country showed that suicide rates were relatively constant; therefore, it must be a social fact that a collective tendency towards suicide existed. These collective tendencies could be related to sets of causes to produce a classification of types of suicide. The sets of causes were theoretically postulated on the basis of Durkheim's conception of possible imbalances between centrifugal forces (too much individualism) and centripetal forces (too much social pressure).

Two pairs of imbalances of forces are defined; one pair refers to the degree of integration or interaction in a group (egoism and altruism), the other pair refers to the degree of moral regulation (anomie and fatalism). The two continua of integration and regulation, and the four types of suicide, can be illustrated in Fig. 3.2 and summary:

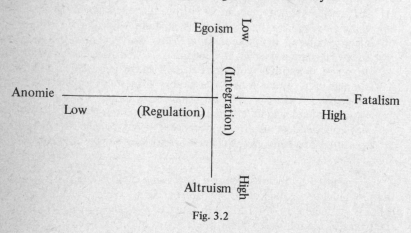

Fig. 3.2

The first type of suicide, at the low extreme of the integration continuum, was *egoistic suicide.* Here rates of interaction in egoistic groups were low, and so values, beliefs, traditions, and sentiments were not held in common by all members. The result was that they weakened each other whenever they came into conflict. The collective life was diminished and individual interests were asserted. The individual lost the beneficial effects of group membership, such as support and revitalization, and consequently found little meaning in group life. Thus suicide rates were higher for Protestants than Catholics, both in comparisons between predominantly Protestant countries and Catholic countries, and between Protestants and Catholics in the same society. It was not the case that one religion's beliefs condemned suicide and the other did not, as suicide was severely condemned by both Protestantism and Catholicism. The difference was that Protestanism encouraged individual free inquiry and, unlike Catholicism, it did not offer priestly and sacramental supports. Where a Protestant church did offer more of those supports, as in the Church of England, which had kept some of the Catholic emphasis on priesthood and sacraments (and had more clergyman per head of population than Protestant countries) the suicide rate was mid-way between that of the Catholic and Protestant countries.

A further example of egoistic suicide was the higher rate to be found among adults who were unmarried compared with married people of the same age. And the larger the family, the lower was the chance of suicide occurring. Finally egoistic suicide varied inversely with the degree of political integration, the rate fell in wars and political crises.

Altruistic suicide was the result of too much integration. The individual absorbed and controlled by the group had an under-developed and so under-valued sense of individuality. Such a person could not resist the pressure to sacrifice the self for the group's interests, even if it meant committing suicide. Durkheim pointed out the similarity of the modern army and primitive society in this respect; in both there was a lack of individuality and a strong pressure towards self-sacrifice. Examples of suicides in primitive societies included suicides of the old or very ill, suicides of women on their husbands' death, and suicides of followers or servants on the death of their chiefs. The much higher rate of military suicides compared with civilians in modern suicide was explained by Durkheim in terms of military morality being a survival of primitive morality, predisposing the soldier to kill himself "at the least disappointment, for the most futile reasons, for a refusal of leave, a reprimand, an unjust punishment, a delay in promotion, a question of honour, a flush of momentary jealousy, or even simply because other suicides have occurred before his eyes or to his knowledge" [1] p. 239.

The next type of suicide, at the low extreme of the regulation continuum, was *anomic suicide*. Anomie was the consequence of social change resulting in a diminution of social regulation. He discussed two forms of economic anomie — "acute" and "chronic", and then "chronic domestic" anomie. They were all cases of an imbalance between means and needs — states of disequilibrium, where means were inadequate to fulfil needs. Durkheim did not believe that needs were given in man's biological, psychological, or individual nature. Indeed, that was one of his main criticisms of the economic, psychological, and utilitarian theories of his time, because they ignored the socially-derived and variable nature of human needs. Passions, desires, appetites, ends, and goals could all become needs, and if such wants were not restrained they would bring unhappiness. The individual's wants were boundless unless a limit was set on them by an external moral authority.

Acute economic anomie occurred in booms and slumps. In both circumstances old rules relating means to ends were inapplicable, and individuals were freed from social restraint, creating disequilibrium, unhappiness, and leading to an increase in suicides. *Chronic economic anomie* was a product of a longer term diminution of social regulation of the relation between means and ends. For over a century there had been an erosion of the influence of agencies that had exercised moral restraint over economic relations, particularly religious and occupational groups, and instead of being regarded as a means, industry had become an end in itself. Not surprisingly, suicide rates were higher in manufacturing and commercial occupations than they were in agriculture, because the latter still had traditions and customs that exercised constraint. (Not that Durkheim wanted to revert to older forms of organization, although he believed new occupational associations should be formed that would have some of the same functions as the old guilds.) Constant economic striving after limitless goals could not bring happiness, as was shown by the fact that the higher socio-economic strata had higher rates of suicide than the poor.

Acute domestic anomie was exemplified by widowhood, which represented a crisis for the surviving husband or wife, who would not be adapted to the new situation and so offered less resistance to suicide.

Chronic domestic anomie was discussed by Durkheim in terms of the way in which marital regulation affects the means–needs balance in men and women. He defined marriage as: "A regulation of sexual relations, including not merely the physical instincts which this intercourse involves but the feelings of every sort gradually engrafted by civilization on the foundation of physical desire" [1], p. 270. Civilization had produced a multiplicity of triggers of man's passions, and only marriage could channel those needs within attainable bounds; bachelors, however, experience limitless horizons, which lead to unrestrained passions that create a disjunction between means and ends, and a state of chronic anomie. Consequently, bachelors had a higher suicide rate than married men. Ease of divorce had a similar effect on married men, producing higher suicide rates. Women, who had long been more restricted within the domestic sphere, had not had their sexual aspirations raised to the same level, and so they required less regulation. Marriage served to over-regulate them, particularly if it was difficult to secure a divorce (they had a lower rate of suicide in societies where divorce was easier than in those where it was difficult). As distinct from family life with children, marriage itself offered no protection against suicidal pressures so far as women were concerned. The interests of the two sexes were in conflict:

> "Speaking generally, we now have the cause of that antagonism of the sexes which prevents marriage favouring them equally: their interests are contrary; one needs restraint and the other liberty. ... Women can suffer more from marriage if it is unfavourable to her than she can benefit by it if it conforms to her interest. This is because she has less need of it" [1], p. 274-275.

Fatalistic suicide was at the high extreme of the regulation continuum. He only discussed this condition of excessive regulation once, and that was restricted to an eight-sentence footnote. Examples were the situation of childless married women (presumably where divorce was difficult), young husbands, and slaves. He described it as the suicide of "persons with futures pitilessly blocked. . . . or all suicides attributable to excessive physical or moral despotism." For some reason, not specified, he decided that "it has so little contemporary importance, and examples are so hard to find aside from the cases just mentioned, that it seems useless to dwell upon it" [1], p. 276, footnote 25.

Although Durkheim used the categories of egoism, altruism, and anomie (not so much fatalism) to distinguish suicidogenic currents, and collective tendencies, he admitted that in practice it was very difficult to separate the currents of egoism and anomie as they flowed from a single source — the loss of mechanical solidarity and the failure to develop a genuine organic solidarity. A moderate amount of egoism and anomie was necessary for progress. A certain amount of individualism was necessary for the growth of the division of labour; it was excessive egoistic tendencies that produced a pathological level of egoistic suicides. Similarly, with anomie, "among peoples where progress is and should be rapid, rules restraining individuals must be sufficiently pliable and malleable; if they preserved all the rigidity they possess in primitive societies, evolution thus impeded could not take place promptly enough" [1] , p. 364.

The language of forces and currents in states of disequilibrium was symptomatic of Durkheim's effort to demonstrate that a sociological explanation of suicide could reveal hidden causes — in this case social forces that were as real as physical forces. Although his references to suicidogenic currents sound like an over-drawn analogy with electrical currents, in fact they refer to phenomena specified in his multi-layered model. Such theoretically conceptualized phenomena were quite different from those given to us by common sense and direct observation: "If we had really only to open our eyes and take a good look to perceive at once the laws of the social world, sociology would be useless or, at least very simple"[1], p. 311. He answered the objection that "since there is nothing in society except individuals, how could there be anything external to them?", by outlining the various levels of social phenomena that exerted a determining force over the individual and that alone could account for the common cause that produced stable rates of suicide. The layers of social phenomena included material facts (architecture, communication and transportation channels, technology, language, etc.). "Social life, which is thus crystallized, as it were, and fixed on material supports, is by just so much externalized, and acts upon us from without"[1], p. 314. The same characteristics were shared by dogmas of faith and legal precepts, especially if they assumed a material form by being written down. And then there was the layer of more fluid and less crystallized or less firmly structured currents of opinion, sentiment, and feeling, which articulated with the other layers of phenomena in various ways, and which constituted the social psychological processes that gave rise to suicidogenic currents. Some currents were feeble or cancelled each other out. It was the sum of the tendencies that had to be taken into consideration, not the individual tendencies:

"No moral idea exists which does not combine in proportions varying with the society involved, egoism, altruism, and a certain anomie. For social life assumes both that the individual has a certain personality, that he is ready to surrender it if the community requires, and finally, that he is to a certain degree sensitive to ideas of progress. This is why there is no people among whom these three currents of opinion do not co-exist, bending men's inclinations in three different and even opposing directions. Where they offset one another, the moral agent is in a state of equilibrium which shelters him against any thought of suicide. But let one of them exceed a certain strength to the detriment of the others, and as it becomes individualized, it also becomes suicidogenic, for the reasons assigned"[1], p. 321.

The strength of these currents depended on three sorts of causes:

"(1) the nature of the individuals composing the society; (2) the manner of their association, that is, the nature of the social organization; (3) the transitory occurrences which disturb the functioning of the collective life without changing its anatomical constitution, such as national crises, economic crises, etc." (ibid).

The first factor, individual characteristics, did not affect suicide rates much because individual differences tended to cancel each other out. It was only when certain characteristics became general that they affected suicide rates, and this sort of predisposing characteristic was usually a product of the second factor — the type of social organization and its associated culture. The fact that suicide rates had trebled, quadrupled, and even quintupled in some countries, in less than fifty years, meant that: "Our social organization, then, must have changed profoundly in the course of this century, to have been able to cause such a growth in the suicide rate"[1], pp. 378-9.

Old forms of organization which had integrated individuals and regulated means-end relationships had declined and disintegrated (e.g. family, Church, occupational guilds, etc.). No adequate functional substitutes had been developed, and so there were pathological states of social disequilibrium, of which suicide rates were a symptom.

The final chapter of the book, titled "Practical Consequences", discussed those institutional developments and some possible remedies. Contrary to many popular misconceptions about Durkheim's political diagnoses, which tend to suggest that he was essentially conservative because he recommended moral renewal and neglected the need for structural change, this chapter made it plain that this was not the case. The Third Republic made education its central instrument of social change, and Durkheim was dedicated to that project, but he rejected the idea that education could cure the ills of society unless there were deeper structural reforms, particularly in the economic sphere. He discussed the argument in favour of education as a cure for suicide and other social ills, and concluded:

"But this is to ascribe to education a power it lacks. It is only the image and reflection of society. It imitates and reproduces the latter in abbreviated form; it does not create it. Education is healthy when people themselves are in a healthy state; but it becomes corrupt with them, being unable to modify itself. . . . The strongest wills cannot elicit non-existent forces from nothingness, and the shocks of experience constantly dissipate these facile illusions. Besides, even though through some incomprehensible miracle a pedagogical system were constituted in opposition to the social system, this very antagonism would rob it of all effect

. . . . Education, therefore, can be reformed only if society itself is reformed. To do that, the evil from which it suffers must be attacked at its source"[1], p. 372-3.

"Is the evil then incurable?" Durkheim asked. His answer was that it need not be so, as his sociological analysis had disclosed the underlying causes of the disease. What was required on the constructive side was a new form of social organization in the economic sphere, which was the main source of the crisis. It could take the form of occupational guilds, which would manage their sector of the economy, fixing prices and wages, providing for the social welfare of their members and their families, fixing contracts and standards, and acting "in the name of the common interest to prevent the strong from unduly exploiting the weak"[1], p. 380. In addition to this positive reform, structural sources of inequality and exploitation would have to be removed, as he made clear in his discussion of the forced division of labour and in later writings on the state and politics (especially *Professional Ethics and Civic Morals*).

Like Marx in his analysis of the causes of alienation, deriving from the mode of the division of labour, Durkheim believed that his scientific analysis of suicide had uncovered the structural forces that caused anomie and egoism, and these too were pathological features of the course taken by the division of labour. Unlike Marx, partly because they were writing in different historical periods in the development of capitalism, and also because they had different views about human nature, Durkheim criticized the amoral characteristics of the existing social organization, which affected *all* social classes. Their higher suicide rates showed that the rich were also victims of these structural pressures, just as the poor suffered in other respects. None of these consequences were intended or willed, they were unintended consequences of human actions; that was why it was essential for scientific sociology to disclose the underlying structural forces that produced these effects.

3.6.2 Criticisms and developments of Durkheim's argument
There are many criticisms of Durkheim's findings regarding specific variables affecting suicide rates, which is not surprising as his work inspired considerable sociological research on the subject. However, despite the many specific criticisms of his work, it has been highly praised by mathematical sociologists for its imaginative use of the available statistics, and more generally for its brilliant linking of theory and empirical data. The more serious criticisms concern his conceptu-

alization and argument, such as his argument by elimination of alternative explanations, his attempt to exclude subjective elements from his
definition of suicide and its causes, and the fuzziness of the distinction
between egoistic and anomic suicide (cf. Pope, [2]).

In retrospect, there can be no doubt that his effort to establish the
scientific status of sociological explanation led him into excesses in
argument, especially in his claim that by showing the insufficiences of
explanations of suicide that referred to non-social factors (race, climate,
insanity, the psychological process of imitation, etc.) he thereby
established the sole validity of his own explanation. It would have been
sufficient for him to rest his case on the proven need to *also* include
social factors as part of any comprehensive explanation of suicide and
suicide rates. Today, a sociologist would have no difficulty in accepting
that some of these different explanations can be complementary,
particularly psychological explanations which can help to determine
why certain individuals commit suicide whereas others do not, although
they may be in similar social circumstances. Many sociologists would
also wish to include references to subjective factors, such as values and
motivation, in their definitions and explanations of suicide. Indeed,
it is now recognized that official statistics of suicide are based on
judgements by officials, such as coroners, concerning the intent of
the victim. Although Durkheim ruled out the use of intent and motive
in developing a definition of suicide, the conventional definition
employed by court officials was "the intentional taking of one's own
life".

Therefore, the very statistics Durkheim was using were based on
conjectures about subjective factors. Furthermore, critics have pointed
out, there were probably systematic biases in the recording of deaths as
suicide, and these could vary between countries and with regard to
different groups — the rich and influential probably having more
capacity to secure less embarrassing verdicts. Douglas [3] cited figures
suggesting that the number of recorded suicides in various European
countries increased when secular officials replaced religious function-
aries as those responsible for recording cause of death. Other sociologists who have done research on coroners' decisions on suicides
find that coroners operate with a "commonsense theory" of suicide —
if the information on a dead person fits into the particular theory,
then the death is more likely to be categorized as suicide. Unlike
Durkheim's "realist" approach, which takes statistics to correspond to a
social fact — a real rate of suicide, these more "phenomenological"
approaches to the study of suicide focus on the meanings and assumptions of those who define acts as suicide, such as coroners. Not surpris-

ingly, sociologists who adopt this approach are critical of Durkheim; others, who continue to use official statistics in their sociological comparisons of suicide rates, are more likely to be critical of Durkheim on the details of his analysis, whilst admiring his pioneering example.

In fact, Durkheim was not unaware of the effects of subjective judgements by officials responsible for classifying deaths as suicides. He discussed this problem when giving reasons for developing his own theoretically-derived classification of types of suicide in preference to the classification used in some countries, where officials made guesses about the motives of victims, such as family trouble, physical or other pain, remorse, drunkenness, etc. He maintained that "what are called statistics of the motives of suicide are actually statistics of the opinions concerning such motives of officials, often of lower officials in charge of the information service"[1], p. 148. Thus it was a matter of degree of reliability or unreliability of specific statistics that had to be judged by the sociologist. His analysis showed that in the case of these official classifications of types of suicide based on the attribution of motives, the unreliability was easy to establish because the proportions allocated to each category seldom varied even when there was a considerable increase in the total number of suicides, and there was no variation between sexes or occupations. Durkheim was also aware of the possibility of the reliability of statistics varying from one country to another due to social biases that could affect decisions as to whether a death was classified as suicide or an accident. When comparing the lower rate of England with another Protestant country, Germany, in order to make the point about the more integrating effect of the Church of England compared with other Protestant churches, he noted:

"To be sure, the statistics of English suicides are not very exact. Because of the penalties attached to suicide, many cases are reported as accidental death. However, this inexactitude is not enough to explain the extent of the difference between this country and Germany"[1], p. 160, footnote 6.

Considering that Durkheim did not have at his disposal the computers and statistical tests of reliability that are available to contemporary sociologists, his marshalling and manipulation of data are still worthy of our admiration. And we have seen that he was not unware of the limitations of the data he was using. He would not have been surprised to hear that further work has led to modifications in his findings about specific correlations between various social factors and suicide rates.

The more important criticisms of Durkheim's study of suicide are those directed at questioning its theoretical adequacy. The core of his theory was concerned with analysing types of social solicarity. In the *Division of Labour* he had made a broad contrast between two types of solidarity — one based on resemblance (lack of wide differences between the functions and mentalities of members of a society), which he called "mechanical solidarity"; the other, "organic solidarity" based on interdependence or complementarity (with greater differences between specialized roles and members bound together by a sense of mutual dependence). In *Suicide,* Durkheim recognized the pathological effects of the over-rapid and forced nature of the growth of division of labour, and the consequent failure to develop a true mutualism. This manifested itself in two forms: people were not integrated into group relations of interdependence (egoism), and/or appropriate norms had failed to emerge to promote and regulate group relations (anomie). The important step forward in *Suicide* was that Durkheim attempted to show the consequences of these pathological states for the individual, and also sketched out the social psychological processes by which imbalances in social forces led to egoistic or anomic suicides. In the case of egoistic suicide, lack of integration gave rise to meaninglessness and so to states of apathy, melancholy, and depression. In anomic suicide, insufficient regulation had left individual passions and wants unchecked, leading to irritation, disgust, anger, disappointment, or recrimination. Unfortunately, although he maintained that one of his chief contributions in *Suicide* would be to distinguish between types of suicide, whereas most previous explanations had been inadequate because they assumed that all suicides were the same (e.g. insane acts, sinful acts, etc.), and that he would make the distinction in terms of different sets of causal factors, the distinction remains unclear.

He had established his case that suicide varies inversely with the degree of integration of a society so far as the examples of both egoistic and anomic suicides were concerned, but he had not provided the same statistical demonstration that egoistical suicides were not caused by the same factors as anomic suicides, and *vice versa*. He did not control regulation factors when testing the effect of variations in integration factors, and *vice versa*. For example, in assessing the relationship between integration and suicide by comparing Protestants and Catholics, if normative regulation is the other likely causal factor then it would have to be held constant (i.e. compare only Protestants and Catholics at the same level of regulation) in order to establish the independent effect of integration. In practice, Durkheim frequently implied that integration and regulation were the same thing, referring to their "peculiar affinity" (p. 288), suggesting that egoism and anomie were "usually merely two different aspects of one social state" (ibid), with an "identical cause" (p. 382). And he offered one solution for both — new occupational guilds or corporations. This was all consistent with his basic theory as it unfolded, which was that a normal level of social integration depended on the achievement of a state of equilibrium between the social forces generated by the various layers of social phenomena as they exercised constraint (regulation) over individual behaviour. This thesis had been demonstrated with great cogency in *Suicide,* even if the subsidiary thesis about the distinction between egoistic and anomic suicide had not been substantiated.

3.6.3   Anomie and Deviance

The American sociologist, Robert K. Merton, was responsible for giving a new impetus to the sociological application of Durkheim's concept of anomie, particularly with regard to the explanation of deviant behaviour other than suicide [4]. He elaborated one possible line of development of Durkheim's conceptualization of anomie as disequilibrium in the relations between means and ends (Merton calls these "goals") due to inadequate normative regulation. Merton was mainly concerned with American society, where he detected a universal cultural goal of material success, an unequal distribution of the acceptable means to reach such a goal, and consequent adoption of alternative, illegitimate solutions. His interest was in the structural causes of non-conformist (deviant) behaviour. He analysed this in terms of individual adaptation, using the following typology:

A Typology of Modes of Individual Adaptation

Modes of adaptation	Culture goals	Institutionalized means
1. Conformity	+	+
2. Innovation	+	—
3. Ritualism	—	+
4. Retreatism	—	—
5. Rebellion	±	±

+   Signifies acceptance
—   Signifies rejection
±   Signifies rejection of prevailing values and substitution of new values

[From (Merton, (1957), 1968 edn. p. 194)]

Although Merton's elaboration and application of the concept of anomie was extremely influential, especially in American sociology's studies of deviance, it changed the emphasis that the concept had in Durkheim's own work. It also lost the critical nature of the concept as Durkheim had intended it, and gave the impression that he was only concerned with problems of nonconformity. Merton did not simply extend Durkheim's concept, but transformed it. Whereas Durkheim had examined normlessness as a condition of imbalance due to the absence of agreed social value (i.e. social goals), for Merton the emphasis was on normlessness in respect to means. Merton saw crime and deviance as the consequences of strains produced by differentiated access to the means to attain commonly held goals. Strain and anomie were induced by strongly defined goals and weakly defined means of attaining these goals. But for Durkheim, anomie was not produced by the combination of strong culture and weak means, but by the weakness of culture due to inadequacies in the social structure (e.g. forced division of labour, lack of morally legitimate forms of economic association). Anomie was weak culture that failed to define the goals of human endeavour, leaving only insatiable greed, and the meaninglessness that led to despair and suicide, rather than crime and deviance.

REFERENCES

[1] Emile Durkheim, *Suicide,* trs. J. A. Spaulding and G. Simpson, Glencoe, Illinois, Free Press, 1951.

[2] Whitney Pope, *Durkheim's Suicide: A Classic Analyzed*, Chicago, University of Chicago Press, 1976.

[3] J. D. Douglas, *The Social Meanings of Suicide,* Princeton, Princeton University Press, 1967.

[4] Robert K. Merton, *Social Theory and Social Structure,* Glencoe, Illionois, Free Press, 1957, new enlarged edition 1968.

3.7 RELIGION AND KNOWLEDGE – THE ELEMENTARY FORMS OF THE RELIGIOUS LIFE

3.7.1 Character and content of the argument

The Elementary Forms of the Religious Life [1] was the last of Durkheim's major works published in his lifetime. Its differed from *Suicide* in that, whereas the latter work had made extensive comparisons using statistics, the *Elementary Forms* adopted the method of in-depth examination of one good case in order to develop a thesis. The case chosen was that of totemic religion in a clan-based society, the Australian aborigines. The reason for this was that these represented the most elementary forms of religion and social organization, in Durkheim's view. If an explanation could be found for the relations between the most sacred elements of social life and the most mundane aspects, and if principles of structural correspondence could be discerned linking the two sets of phenomena, then sociologists would have the key to understanding the originating principles of phenomena in our own more complex societies. The phenomena that would be explained would be "ideological" in various senses of that term. One important sense was that of "misrecognition" of itself by society, in that members were given an idealized view of society, which had its origins in elevated and awe-inspiring experiences of great periodic gatherings of a religious or socio-political nature. Among the typical products of such ideological idealization and sanctification were the authority attributed to political leaders, and the sense of "oneness" and belonging (as in nationalism and patriotism). From his discussion of primitive religion Durkheim aimed to show the social origins of all categories of thought — cognitive, evaluative, and the emotionally expressive. It can be seen that the *Elementary Forms* was the most ambitious of all Durkheim's works.

Religious institutions — beliefs and practices — could not be dismissively explained as a complete fantasy, corresponding to nothing in reality. Sociologists, in particular, could not hold such a point of view:

> "In fact, it is an essential postulate of sociology that a human institution cannot rest upon an error and a lie, without which it could not exist. . . . When only the letter of the formulae is considered, these religious beliefs and practices undoubtedly seem disconcerting at times, and one is tempted to attribute them to some sort of deep-rooted error. But one must know how to go underneath the symbol to the reality which it represents and which gives it its meaning. The most barbarous and the most fantastic rites and the strangest myths translate some human need, some aspect of life, either individual or social. The reasons with which the faithful justify them may be, and generally are, erroneous; but the true reasons do not cease to exist, and it is the duty of science to discover them. In reality, then, there are no religions which are false. All are true in their own fashion; all answer, though in different ways, to the given conditions of human existence"[1], pp. 14-15.

The next point was that, in order to understand an existing ideology, whether it related to religion, politics, economics, or any other institution, it was necessary to trace its historical development, which had produced the present layers and combinations of elements. It should not be thought that there will be a direct correspondence between ideology and existing social structure; ideology is a historical product:

"In the first place, we cannot arrive at an understanding of the most recent religions except by following the manner in which they have been progressively composed in history. In fact, historical analysis is the only means of explanation which it is possible to apply to them. It alone enables us to resolve an institution into its constituent elements, for it shows them to us as they are born in time, one after another. On the other hand, by placing every one of them in the condition where it was born, it puts into our hands the only means we have of determining the causes which gave rise to it. Every time we undertake to explain something human, taken at a given moment in history — be it a religious belief, a moral precept, a legal principle, an aesthetic style, or an economic system — it is necessary to commence by going back to its most primitive and simple form, to try to account for the characteristics by which it was marked at that time, and then to show how it developed and became complicated little by little, and how it became that which it is at the moment in question"[1], p. 15.

Durkheim posited certain basic characteristics and functions of religion, even though the forms of religion might vary in specific cases:

"At the foundation of all systems of beliefs and of all cults there ought necessarily to be a certain number of fundamental represent- ations or conceptions and of ritual attitudes which, in spite of the diversity of forms which they have taken, have the same objective significance and fulfil the same functions everywhere"[1], p. 17.

It made methodological sense to try to discern these in simpler forms of religion to start with, because in complex religions it would be difficult to distinguish secondary from principal elements. The great religions of Egypt, India, and classical antiquity were "a confused mass of many cults, varying according to the locality, the temples, the generations, the dynasties, the invasions, etc. Popular superstitions are there confused with the purest dogma" (ibid.).

In simpler societies the fundamental elements and relations were closer to their original form, and so there was less to strip off in the way of accretions and fewer transformations to trace back. For this reason, "Primitive civilizations offer privileged cases, then, because they are simple cases"[1], p. 18. And furthermore, "primitive religions do not merely aid us in disengaging the constituent elements of religion; they also have the great advantage that they facilitate the explanation of it. Since the facts there are simpler, the relations between them are more apparent"[1], p. 19.

In a sense he was taking up the old question of the origins of religion, which had engaged theologians and philosophers for hundred of years, but he was recasting it in a new form and with a different methodology:

"To be sure, if by origin we are to understand the very first beginning, the question has nothing scientific about it, and should be resolutely discarded. There was no given moment when religion began to exist, and there is consequently no need of finding a means of transporting ourselves thither in thought. Like every human institution, religion did not commence anywhere. Therefore, all speculations of this sort are justly discredited; they can only consist in subjective and arbitrary constructions which are subject to no sort of control. But the problem which we raise is quite another one. What we want to do is to find a means of discerning the ever-present causes upon which the most essential forms of religious thought and practice depend"[1], p. 20.

Durkheim's confidence in the explanatory powers of sociology, and in its ability to secure new data through ethnography, had grown considerably since his early days at Bordeaux. From the 1890s onwards ethnographers' published findings on simpler societies, such as those in Australia and the Indians of North America, reached impressive proportions. Durkheim and his colleagues on L'Année sociologique had applied their sociological methodology to the analysis of those materials and built up a reputation for expertise in such matters. Consequently, although Durkheim focused on religion, it was viewed by him as part of a larger project. His intention was to demonstrate that sociology could provide an answer to questions that previously had been asked by philosophers — questions about the bases of knowledge itself. If it could be shown that religious cosmologies were the most primitive ways of ordering man's view of his world, and that those cosmologies, which were socially-derived, gave rise to the categories that structured other types of knowledge, then the sociology of knowledge would be firmly established. His Introduction to the Elementary Forms made it clear that this was the larger case he wished to argue:

"But our study is not of interest merely for the science of religion. In fact, every religion has one side by which it overlaps the circle of properly religious ideas, and there, the study of religious phenomena gives a means of renewing the problems which, up to the present, have only been discussed among philosophers. For a long time it has been known that the first systems of representations with which men have pictured to themselves the world and themselves were of religious origin. There is no religion that is not a cosmology at the same time that it is a speculation upon divine things. If philosophy and the sciences were born of religion, it is because religion began by taking the place of the sciences and philosophy. . . . Men owe to it not only a good part of the substance of their knowledge, but also the form in which this knowledge has been elaborated. At the roots of all our judgements there are a certain number of essential ideas which dominate all our intellectual life; they are what philosophers since Aristotle have called the categories of the understanding: ideas of time, space, class, number, cause, substance, personality, etc. They correspond to the most universal properties of things. . . . They are like the framework of the intelligence. Now when primitive religious beliefs are systematically analyzed, the principal categories are naturally found. They are born in religion and of religion; they are a product of religious thought"[1], pp. 21-2.

He summarized the thesis of the book in the following paragraph of the Introduction:

"The general conclusion of the book which the reader has before him is that religion is something eminently social. Religious representations are collective representations which express collective realities; the rites are a manner of acting which take rise in the midst of the assembled groups and which are destined to excite, maintain, or recreate certain mental states in these groups. So if the categories are of religious origin, they ought to participate in this nature common to all religious facts; they should be social affairs and the product of collective thought. At least — for in the actual condition of our knowledge of these matters, one should be careful to avoid all radical and exclusive statements — it is allowable to suppose that they are rich in social elements"[1], p. 22.

He adopted his usual procedure in arguing this thesis. Firstly, he examined and eliminated existing alternative theories and definitions.

Once again he attacked psychological theories and those based on supposed mental qualities and processes in the individual. He was especially critical of what he regarded as the most common form of such explanations, which said that religion was belief in the supernatural, and that people believed in the supernatural in order to explain things which surpassed the limits of their knowledge and understanding.

This common assumption about religion was born out of modern man's sense of superiority with regard to his predecessors; he could not understand how earlier people had believed such things, unless it was simply a matter of ignorance and inability to find rational explanations for things they experienced. But, said Durkheim, primitive man had no such experience of having to resort to postulating a supernatural realm in order to explain puzzling or awe-inspiring phenomena in nature. There is no evidence that they found such things in the least puzzling, nor did the awareness that there was a "natural order of things" distinct from a supernatural order arise until modern science made us aware of it. With a certain touch of irony, he added that this should not be too difficult for us to understand, because even now many of our contemporaries retain a primitive conception of *social* facts, believing "that a legislator can create an institution out of nothing by a mere injunction of its will, or transform one social system into another", just as religious people believed God created the world out of nothing. The principle of determinism and the scientific method had only recently been adopted in the study of society, and many people had still not accepted the need for such a science. If our contemporaries still retained an

"antiquated conception for sociological affairs, it is not because the life of societies appears obscure and mysterious to them; on the contrary, if they are so easily contented with these explanations, and if they are so obstinate in their illusions which experience constantly belies, it is because social events seem to them the clearest thing in the world; it is because they have not yet realized their real obscurity; it is because they have not yet recognized the necessity of resorting to the laborious methods of the natural sciences to gradually scatter the darkness. The same state of mind is to be found at the root of many religious beliefs which surprise us by their pseudo-simplicity. It is science and not religion which has taught men that things are complex and difficult to understand" [1], pp. 41-2.

The definition and explanation of religious phenomena was not to be sought in their content, such as a supernatural element, but in the characteristic attitude of people toward certain phenomena which set them apart from other phenomena. The contents of religious beliefs, and the choice of some things and not others to be regarded with religious veneration, were infinitely varied. Some religions, according to Durkheim, did not contain references to a supernatural agency; he mentioned Buddhism as an example. (He recognized that certain versions of Buddhism did contain such references, and also that Buddhists did not deny the existence of divinities, but simply were not concerned about whether they existed.) Furthermore, even in religions which did contain theistic beliefs, there were many religious rites which had no discernible connection with those theistic beliefs. In the Bible,

"it is forbidden to hitch an ass and a horse together, or to wear a garment in which the hemp is mixed with flax, but it is impossible to see the part which belief in Jahveh can have played in these interdictions, for he is wholly absent from all the relations thus forbidden, and could not be interested in them"(Ibid, p. 49).

Thus, it cannot be said that the focal point of all religious phenomena is God or the supernatural:

"there are rites without gods, and even rites from which gods are derived. . . . Religion is more than the idea of gods or spirits, and consequently cannot be defined exclusively in relation to these latter"[1], p. 50.

Durkheim divided religious phenomena into two fundamental categories: beliefs and rites. "The first are states of opinion, and consist in representations; the second are determined modes of action"[1], p. 51. Rites could be defined and distinguished from other practices, such as moral practices, by the special nature of their object. That special nature of the object was expressed in beliefs, and all religious beliefs had a common characteristic:

"All known religious beliefs, whether simple or complex, present one common characteristic: they presuppose a classification of all the things, real and ideal, of which men think, into two classes or opposed groups, generally designated by two distinct terms which are translated well enough by the words *profane* and *sacred*. This division of the world into two domains, the one containing all that is sacred, the other all that is profane, is the distinctive trait of religious thought; the beliefs, myths, dogmas, and legends are either representations or systems of representations which express the nature of sacred things, the virtues and powers which are attributed to them, or their relations with each other and with profane things"[1] , p. 52.

The fallacy of animistic and naturalistic theories of religion, which were so popular among early anthroplogists and sociologists, such as Tylor and Spencer, was that they located the origin of religious sentiments in psychological phenomena (such as dreams) or in natural wonders (such as storms). Durkheim thought this put the cart before the horse. The idea that dreams could be interpreted and that natural objects could express the divinity, was socially learned; it was as much the effect of religion as the cause of it. It was a naive psychologism, as propounded by Spencer, that explained human belief in the soul as having originated in dream and trance experiences during which an individual seemed to be in two places at once. It supposed religion to be an illusion with no real foundation in social life. The belief in the soul, like all religious beliefs, corresponded to something real: it was a symbolic representation of the relation between the individual and society. The soul was that part of society within the individual; it was the moral authority of society that was the objective referent behind the idea of the soul. "Although our moral conscience is a part of our consciousness, we do not feel ourselves on an equality with it"[1], p. 298.

The moral ascendancy of society over the individual was the source of the sacred attitude, by which certain things were regarded as symbols of a morally superior, and so sacred, force.

However, it was not simply a matter of hierarchy, with the inferior dependent on the superior, that distinguished the sacred from the profane. There were many hierachical relationships in society that were not sacred. And many things that were sacred did excite great respect, e.g. an amulet. Even the relationship with gods was often one of reciprocity and mutual dependence; some religions believed the god would die if denied offerings and sacrifices. It was the absolute distinction between the sacred and the profane, their logical opposition, that provided the criterion of religious beliefs.

"The sacred thing is *par excellence* that which the profane should not touch, and cannot touch with impunity. To be sure, this interdiction cannot go so far as to make all communication between the two worlds impossible; for if the profane could in no way enter into relations with the sacred, this latter could be good for nothing" [1] , p. 55.

This notion of a system of classification based on fundamental opposition between two classes, which nevertheless need each other, was the core idea in the various versions of structuralism developed by sociologists and anthropologists inspired by Durkheim, such as Claude Lévi-Strauss and Mary Douglas, [2, 3].

Durkheim's definition of religion was not complete with his description of it as a system of relations based on the opposition of the sacred and the profane. Magic, too, was made up of beliefs and rites, some of which resembled religion. But magic was not the same as religion; it was more likely to be used for purely technical and utilitarian ends (e.g. it sought to manipulate supernatural forces to produce rain, rather than praying to God to grant rain), and, more importantly, it did not bind its adherents into a moral community. "The magician has a clientele and not a Church"[1], p. 60. Because of the source of the sacred — the moral superiority of the social — religion was contained in a moral community, which Durkheim called a Church. Thus he arrived at his definition of religion:

> "A religion is a unified system of beliefs and practices relative to sacred things, that is to say, things set apart and forbidden — beliefs and practices which unite into one single moral community called a Church, all those who adhere to them"[1], p. 62.

The case chosen to demonstrate his thesis of the correspondence between religion and society was that of totemic religion in a clan-based society; specifically, the Australian aborigines, supplemented by ethnographic data on certain American Indian societies with a similar structure and totemic religion. In view of the later prominence given to the study of myths using a structuralist method, as in the work of Lévi-Strauss, it must be pointed out that Durkheim considered myths too complex a phenomenon to be studied at this stage, and he proposed to concentrate on the most elementary notions at the basis of the religion — those concerning the cultic rites. Among the most basic concepts of totemism was the identity it established for the clan. Clans were composed of members who considered themselves united by a bond of kinship; but it was not based on blood. The relationship rested on a shared name, and the name was that of the species of material things (the totem) with which the clan believed it had relations of kinship.

The species were usually animals and plants, such as the kangaroo or the crow, and in no sense awe-inspiring or remarkable. Nor could it be said that people worshipped their totem species as though it were a god; rather they regarded it as a brother or sister — they shared kinship with the kangaroo or whichever was their totem. The totem was not a mere name, but contained the distinctive characteristics of the clan. The sacred character of the totem was shared by images of it as inscribed on material artifacts and on the person; the sacred attributes were also shared by the clan members themselves. The same essence, or vital principle, was therefore shared by the totem, images of the totem, and members of the clan. The totem was at once both the symbol of the vital principle (referred to as *mana* in some simple societies) and of the society, because god and society were the same things:

"The god of the clan, the totemic principle, can therefore be nothing else than the clan itself, personified and represented to the imagination under the visible form of the animal or vegetable which serves as its totem"[1], p. 236.

Durkheim posed the question of how this apotheosis had been possible, and how did it happen to take place in this fashion? The answer lay in the feelings of dependency created by the totem and society:

"In a general way, it is unquestionable that a society has all that is necessary to arouse the sensation of the divine in minds, merely by the power that it has over them; for to its members it is what a god is to his worshippers. In fact, a god is, first of all, a being whom men think of as superior to themselves, and upon whom they feel that they depend. . . . Now society also gives us the sensation of a perpetual dependence. . . at every instant we are obliged to submit ourselves to rules of conduct and of thought which we have neither made nor desired, and which are sometimes even contrary to our most fundamental inclinations and instincts"[1], pp. 236-7.

The function of totemism was to bind clan members, who were frequently dispersed in small hordes, in a symbolical unity and in subservience to the collectivity, which exerted a moral authority. It also served to provide the basis of a system of universal classification for the members (a cosmology), which categorized all other phenomena and entities with which they came into contact, including their relations with other clans, especially in the exchange of marriage partners. Thus the thesis on totemism provides the key to explaining the fundamental process of symbolization, the bases of social authority, and the principles regulating relations between social units engaged in exchanges.

It explains symbolization as the way in which a material object can serve to express the clansmen's feelings of dependence on each other and their moral identiy; it allows them to think the complex reality of their social groups in simplified form:

"Now the totem is the flag of the clan. It is therefore natural that the impressions aroused by the clan in individual minds — impressions of dependence and of increased vitality — should fix themselves to the idea of the totem rather than of the clan: for the clan is too complex a reality to be represented clearly in all its complex unity by such rudimentary intelligence. More than that, the primitive does not even see that these impressions come to him from the group"[1], p. 252.

The symbolization arises, fixes itself in the minds and emotions, and is revitalized, at periodic ceremonial and ritual gatherings of exceptional social intensity. The life of the aborigines alternates between two modes: periods of dispersal, when they are engaged in mundane economic activities of "very mediocre intensity"; and the religious gatherings, or a corroboree (when the women and the uninitiated can take part), when there are activities of an exceptional — even deviant — nature, and heightened intensity. An interesting feature of the latter gatherings was that they were dangerously exciting, when the people almost literally "played with fire". Normal rules were broken and feverish activity indulged in that could not be sustained in normal times; it was as though the customary order was smelted in the fire after having been temporarily dissolved:

"They are so far removed from their ordinary conditions of life, and they are so thoroughly conscious of it, that they feel that they must set themselves outside of and above thier ordinary morals. The sexes unite contrarily to the rules governing sexual relations. Men exchange wives with each other. Sometimes even incestuous unions, which in normal times are thought abominable and are severely punished, are now contracted openly and with impunity" [1], p. 247.

The effect of such gatherings was to impress on the members their sense of participation in a larger unity, and their dependence on a superior moral force that saved them from chaos and disorder. Their feeling of being part of a distinctive and sacred unity was stengthened by negative and positive rites; the former were rituals of avoidance and taboo, and the latter were rituals of communion with the divine essence. Negative rites aimed at limiting contact between the sacred and the profane, and prepared the initiate for entry into the sacred domain. The transition from one realm to the other was marked by abstinence, physical ordeals, and the donning of special clothes and ornaments. Positive rites in Australian totemism included ceremonies to ensure the prosperity of the animal or plant that served as the totem, and a concluding ceremony in which the totem was ritually eaten and songs were sung praising the past exploits of human and non-human past members of the clan. The practice of sacrifice in more developed religions was based on the same idea of communion with the divine through eating the flesh (e.g. the Body of Christ symbolized by bread in the Christian Communion Service) and the offering of it to the divinity. A third form of rites were those associated with mourning – "piacular" rites; these were a mixture of negative and positive rites. They included abstaining from certain things, such as economic activity, and observing positive rites like wailing and wearing special clothing. These were not merely an expression of grief, but also a way of drawing the group together when its solidarity was threatened by the loss of a member.

It should be remembered that Durkheim was not analysing these processes in primitive society simply for the sale of understanding those societies and their religion, but in order to get to the roots of social processes and institutions in modern society. The dynamic density of morphological factors that he wrote about in the *Division of Labour* and used as an explanatory factor for social change and new forms of social solidarity, was now supplemented by dynamic density of a social psychological type. The heightened sense of solidarity and dependence created by the effervescence of great collective gatherings, was to be found occurring in revolutonary or creative epochs, such as the French Revolution [1], pp. 240-1, and in periodic gatherings:

"That is why all parties political, economic or confessional, are careful to have periodical reunions where their members may revivify their common faith by manifesting it in common"[1], p. 240.

It explains why the most unremarkable people could become remarkable leaders or tyrants: "Under the influence of the general exaltation, we see the most mediocre and inoffensive bourgeois become either a hero or a butcher"[1], p. 242. And it showed how a civil religion could be created in which society was indeed deified:

"This aptitude of society for setting itself up as a god or for creating gods was never more apparent than during the first years of the French Revolution. At this time, in fact, under the influence of the general enthusiasm, things purely laical by nature were transformed by public opinion into sacred things: these were the Fatherland, Liberty, Reason. A religion tended to become established which had its dogmas, symbols, altars and feasts"[1], pp. 244-5.

This idea of a civil religion has been used by modern sociologists, such as Robert Bellah, to explain the beliefs and ceremonies that unite Americans in devotion to their country and its supposed mission (as celebrated on great civic occasions such as Presidential Inaugurations, and at Thankgiving). (cf. Bellah, [4]). It has also been a fertile idea in the sociological explanation of charismatic movements (an idea also developed by Durkheim's great German contemporary, Max Weber, although neither made reference to the other), and with regard to the roots of nationalism.

The most insightful idea in Durkheim's repertory, as marshalled and applied in the thesis of the *Elementary Forms,* was that of the power of symbolization. The symbols, or collective representations, created a reality, which commanded and received obedience; and the sacred-social force could bestow the full power of itself to elicit respect on the most ordinary things, and its force remained as strong however much it was subdivided:

"Out of the commonest object, they can make a powerful sacred being. Yet the powers which are thus conferred, though purely ideal, act as though they were real; they determine the conduct of men with the same degree of necessity as physical forces. . . . Surely the soldier who falls while defending his flag does not believe that he sacrifices himself for a bit of cloth. This is all because social thought, owing to the imperative authority that is in it, has an efficacy that individual thought could never have; by the power which it has over our minds, it can make us see things in whatever light it pleases; it adds to reality or deducts from it according to the circumstances. Thus there is one division of nature where the formula of idealism is applicable almost to the letter: this is the social kingdom. Here more than anywhere else, the idea is the reality"[1], p. 260.

He added that this did not mean we could free ourselves completely from physical necessities; even in order to express our ideas we needed to fix them upon material things which symbolize them. But this was a long way from the kind of position attributed to material things in determining culture, in doctrines such as those he associated with the name of Marx, or in philosophies which believed ideas were simply a reflection of bodily states and sensations. According to Durkheim, "the world of representations in which social life passes is superimposed upon its material substratum, far from arising from it"[1], p. 307.

This brings us to Durkheim's sociology of knowledge and his attempt to locate the origins of basic categories of knowledge in social experience. He did not deny that material circumstances and the individual's experiences of them had a part to play in the formation of knowledge and categories of knowledge. But he claimed that distinctions given to the senses, such as black in contrast with white, night as distinct from day, etc., simply provided the raw material for categorization, along with objects such as the different species that served as totems, or which were classified in separate groups associated with each totem. It was concepts and categories representing society and its sub-divisions that provided the most clear-cut logical oppositions and dichotomies (ultimately the contrasts of sacred and profane, pure and impure), and these exercised a predominant moulding influence on mental life. Whereas the individual's experience of things was in a constant state of flux, concepts were more fixed, because they came from society, and society, through its culture, outlived individuals. The concept of category itself was not given in the individual mind, as the philosopher Kant had taught, for the individual reacts to a constant flow of experience; it is only society which provides the demarcations that create such categories as those of time, space, class, and cause, and these were derived from the society's own life:

"They not only come from society, but the things which they express are of a social nature. Not only is it society which had founded them, but their contents are the different aspects of the social being; the category of class was at first indistinct from the concept of the human group; it is the rhythm of social life which is at the basis of the category of time; the territory occupied by the society furnished the material for the category of space; it was the collective force which was the prototype of the concept of efficient force, an essential element in the category of causality" [1], p. 488.

The example which Durkheim gave of the origins of spatial divisions was that of the Australian societies where space was conceived as a giant circle, reflecting the shape of the encampment; and the abstract divisions of space mirrored the division of the community circle into clan territories. Similarly, time was categorized on the basis of the periodic ceremonial gatherings (much as our modern calendar is based on the seasons and feast days of the Christian year). The idea of truth, as an impersonal standard, set above individual experiences and preferences, derives from the impersonal character of society itself. It is an idea of fundamental importance for the development of science, and science owes it to religion, which gradually evolved in the direction of the universal and away from the parochial and concrete.

What did Durkheim see as the future of religion? Having shown the pre-eminence of religion in developing the categories that formed the basis of thought in all fields, from politics to science, he concluded:

"Thus there is something eternal in religion which is destined to survive all the particular symbols in which religious thought has successively enveloped itself. There can be no society which does not feel the need of upholding and reaffirming at regular intervals the collective sentiments and the collective ideas which make its unity and its personality" [1], pp. 474-475.

Society would continue to need a functional equivalent of the cultic side of religion, even if the ceremonies and rituals were overtly political rather than religious. Also, there would need to be a functional equivalent of religion to produce the ideals that would unite social groups on a moral basis: the ideals of moral individualism were likely to figure prominently in this, emphasizing respect for the individual. But the cognitive side of religion would increasingly be taken over by science, which employed systematically empirical and critical methods that were absent in religious cosmologies.

Some contemporary sociologists of religion have developed this Durkheimian hypothesis of a trend towards individualism. Peter Berger and Thomas Luckmann have suggested that religious individualism has become the most common form of religion in modern industrialized societies. They maintain that beliefs and sentiments relative to sacred things no longer necessarily unite individuals into a single community or congregation, no matter how similar their systems of beliefs may be. Berger has likened the modern religious scene to the economic marketplace, in which individuals shop around for whatever brand suits their present need, and consequently they feel no particular commitment to other people holding similar beliefs, nor to any organization which claims to incorporate such beliefs. Frequently the very content of the beliefs is individualistic, directed toward enhancing the individual's sense of well-being and self-love. Similarly, not only may the cultural and organizational components of religion be functionally differentiated, but so also may the community and congregational components. Among the Arunta discussed by Durkehim there was but one organization, namely the total society, which provided both religious identity (community) and the setting in which religious ends were sought (congregation). But in modern society, as another American sociologist of religion, Will Herberg, pointed out, a religious community, such as the Jews, Catholics, or Protestants, does not necessarily imply actual affiliation with a particular church. (cf. Berger & Luckmann [5], Berger [6], Herberg [7].)

3.7.2 Summary and criticism
Like *Suicide*, the *Elementary Forms* has been enormously influential within its field of study. It is not possible to summarize all the various specific criticisms that have been made, particularly those emanating from anthropologists and ethnographers who have collected data that contradict Durkheim's findings. Nor will we repeat the criticisms that have been mentioned already concerning Durkheim's style of argument, such as his tendency to seek to establish his own argument's validity by eliminating alternatives, and his argument by *petitio principii,* whereby he assumed that which was supposed to be proved by the subsequent argument. An example of the latter is to be found in his very definition of religion as uniting its adherents into a single moral community, which presupposed one of the central theses of the work; also, his hypothesis that collective effervescences generate religious beliefs and rites, presupposed those beliefs and rites, since the effervescences were expressions of them (this argument would have been better left as an explanation of the way in which a religion was reproduced, rather than of its origination). Durkheim was not above stooping to the device of smuggling in confirmatory evidence for his thesis from another society when he could not find it in the case he was discussing; he tended to do this when supplementing his Australian material with data drawn from the American Indian societies. A particularly damaging piece of evidence against the general validity of his thesis is that there does not seem to be a polarity between the sacred and profane in all religions, even though his definition of religion postulated such an opposition. The Judaeo-Christian tradition makes such a distinction, but the religions of some societies studied by anthropologists have no such strict

opposition, and the two are often found intermingling in everyday life. The British anthropologist, Evans-Pritchard, observed that sacred things may be profane only at some times, as in the case of the Azande, who, when their shrines were not in ritual use, used them as convenient props to rest their spears against [8], p. 65.

Another basic assumption in the thesis has been questioned, and that was his claim that the simplest form of society would have the simplest form of religion, and hence the equation between the clan and the totem. Anthropologists like Evans-Pritchard were able to point out that there were people with a much simpler social organization than the Australians, who did not have totems, although they had religions, and that there were clans with no totems, and people with totems and no clans. This makes all the more questionable Durkheim's evolutionist view that totemism was the elementary form of religion, accompaying the most elementary form of social organization, and that complex societies and their religions were a development from those basic principles. In sum: Durkheim's claims for his thesis were too general and over-ambitious.

However, the methods he employed in developing the sociological analysis of religion have continued to inspire sociologists and scholars in other disciplines. The *Elementary Forms* was his most mature and sophisticated deployment of theoretical strategies for studying the components of his multi-layered model of social phenomena. The model itself constituted a basically structuralist model of social phenomena. Within that structuralist framework he then employed three types of explanation: causal, interpretative, and functionalist. The causal explanations focused on the impact of phenomena at the lower and upper levels of his model (respectively, effervescent currents and morphological factors) in crystallizing phenomena on the middle level (the dogmas and rites of institutionalized religion). The effervescent currents produced by the exceptional intensity of social interaction at the periodic gatherings was one causal factor discussed. The other was the causal connection between the morphological features of social structure and the content of religious beliefs and ritual practices, including the religious origination of classificatory systems.

In his interpretative analyses he sought to relate the various levels of phenomena in terms of a structural correspondence that can be described as "metaphoric parallelism". For example, the religious doctrines about the relations between the individual and the totem (or god) were metaphorical representations of parallel relations between the individual and society. Thus the three basic relationships between god and the individual in religious beliefs symbolized parallel relationships between society and the individual: god was transcendent over the individual; god was immanent in the individual; god occupied a status fundamentally different from that of the individual.

The functional hypotheses concerned the part played by beliefs and rites within the total religious and social system. These social functions were performed by religion in its capacity as a system of communication of ideas and sentiments (cognitive and expressive functions) and as a means of specifying and regulating social relationships. (cf. Lukes [9], pp. 470-2). Symbolism served the function of making society conscious of itself, recreating social sentiments, and classifying and regulating statuses and duties. Because the individual could not live without society — indeed, could not be human without society — these functions were beneficial in integrating the individual into society. There is little if any mention of negative effects or dysfunctions of religion in Durkheim's sociology. To some sociologists that is the most serious criticism they would wish to make against this study, and against his sociology in general. More recently, however, it has begun to be seen that the *Elementary Forms* can be read as an account of the origins of social hierarchy and the maintenance of power in that hierarchy, particularly through the reproduction of an ideological consciousness of itself for society. That consciousness entails a view of power that is a mystification and a misrecognition of the real social conditions of its functioning — it bestows moral authority on leaders, and gives the impression that their superiority descends on them from above rather than depending on the opinions of those below them, and it exaggerates the distance separating them from their fellows. (cf. Lacroix [10]).

3.7.3 Developments and applications of Durkheim's ideas

Rather than conclude our discussion of Durkheim's sociology of religion with a selection of criticisms, it might do greater justice to the fertility of the ideas contained in the *Elementary Forms* if we mention a few of the many works those ideas inspired. Two sets of ideas have been particularly fertile: they are his metaphoric parallelism — the notion that religious beliefs symbolize or model social forces, structures and relationships that condition and compel the action of people in society; and his account of the functions of ritual and shared beliefs in reproducing social solidarity. One of the most radical applications of Durkheim's metaphoric parallelism was carried out by Guy Swanson, who, in a controversial monograph, *The Birth of the Gods* [11], adduced the hypothesis that belief in a high god or monotheistic deity only tends to occur in those societies containing three or more different types of hierarchically ordered sovereign groups. In Swanson's view, the presence of three or more types of soverign groups in a society (i.e. a relatively complex hierarchy of political entities), with one group dominating the others, provides the social conditions that a high god symbolizes or represents. It is a hypothesis that has been much criticized, but it generated further studies along these essentially Durkheimian lines.

We have already mentioned the work of Bellah on civil religion [4]. Although he shows that there is less unanimity as to the location of the "sacred" in modern society, in contrast to the societies discussed by Durkheim, he also makes a good case for finding it embodied in the nation, where nationalist ideology portrays its purposes and goals as sacred and transcendent. Under Durkheimian inspiration, sociologists have identified a range of ritualistic mechanisms employed in the renewal of common political sentiments: national constitutions have been described as totemic documents legitimating political power; and other ritualistic mechanisms analysed include Presidential inaugurations in the United States, national holidays, along with political purges, trials, and witch-hunts. The neo-Durkheimian studies of the ideological functions of purges, trials and witch-hunts, refute the criticism that Durkheim's ideas cannot take account of conflict and conflict-management, which was the unfortunate impression left by effective criticisms of earlier neo-Durkheimian studies, such as the study by Shils and Young [19] of the coronation of Elizabeth II, where it was suggested that the society required rituals to sustain an *existing* core of common values. (See the criticism by Birnbaum [20], and also the somewhat different critique by Abercrombie *et al* [21] of the whole idea that capitalist society needs a dominant ideology).

The sociologist and historian Kai T. Erikson has also applied these Durkheimian ideas in a study of the witch-hunts in seventeenth century Salem, Massachusetts [12]. Using the notion of a *boundary crisis,* Erikson shed further light on the function of public rituals for rejuvenating collective representations (including representations that preserve ideological unity) and revitalizing collective sentiments. Erikson's work was an ingenious combination of Durkheim's ideas on the function of crime, in reaffirming the solidarity of the community, and his sociology of religion. Durkheim had maintained that crime represented acts that violated the collective conscience and elicited the wrath of society. The punishment dealt out as an expression of communal wrath resulted in the reaffirmation of the moral order. Erikson argued that a society need not wait for someone to cross the boundary of its normative order before experiencing the desired backlash of ritualistic frenzy. The effect could be achieved by society moving its moral boundaries, thus creating or manufacturing deviance. Durkheim had concentrated on individuals violating the moral order by offending the collective conscience. Erikson pointed out that the same result could be obtained if society altered its definitions of good and evil and thereby created deviants by labelling individuals as outside the normative boundaries. He thought that something like that had happened when the community of Salem and the authorities of the Massachusetts Bay Colony suddenly began to discover witch-craft where none had existed before. His explanation for this manufacturing of deviance was that the community had experienced an external threat (King Charles II began reviewing claims to landownership in Massachusetts and land disputes broke out). The community responded (unconsciously) to the external threat by creating deviants — moving the moral order — which through the mechanism of public trials, had the effect of ritually reaffirming the threatened social boundries. Other sociologists have gone on to apply this analysis to political phenomena such as the Chinese Cultural Revolution and the Watergate Trial. Durkheim's ideas have travelled a long way from their starting point of Australian totemism; which is as he intended.

3.7.4 Primitive Classification and the Sociology of Knowledge — Criticisms

In the *Elementary Forms* and the essay with Mauss, *Primitive Classification* [13], Durkheim advanced a theory of knowledge that came to be labelled as "sociological Kantianism". Whereas the philosopher Kant had posited that categories were given, *a priori*, in the human mind, and so programmed our perception of the world in terms of categories such as space, time, cause, etc., Durkheim claimed that these categories were socially determined. In addition to the discussion of these ideas in the *Elementary Forms*, the other major statement of them, with more detailed examples, is to be found in the essay, *Primitive Classification*. At the beginning of that work, after giving a brief description of the tribal organization of the Australians, which was sub-divided into moieties, marriage classes, and totemic clans, Durkheim and Mauss assert:

> "All the members of the tribe are classed in this way in definite categories which are enclosed one in the other. *Now the classification of things reproduces this classification of men*"[13], (italics in the original).

This was little more than a statement of correspondence, or parallelism, between conceptual classification and social organization. Later, after describing the classificatory systems of the Zuni and the Sioux indians, the authors used the term "express" to describe the relationship:

> "Thus the two types of classification which we have just studied merely express under different aspects the very societies within which they were elaborated; one was modelled on the jural and religious organization of the tribe, the other on its morphological organization"[13] , p. 66.

Elsewhere, however, especially in the *Elementary Forms,* Durkheim slipped over into making causal statements to the effect that conceptual classifications were caused by social organization: "There are societies in Australia and North America where space is conceived in the form of an immense circle, *because* the camp has a circular form..."[1], p. 24 (italics added). In order to establish such causal relations, Durkheim and Mauss would have had to check concomitant variation — comparing cases where, for example, the camp was in the form of a circle, to see if space was conceived as a circle in all cases, and *vice versa*. In fact, they never looked for contrary cases.

One of the main criticisms of Durkheim's sociology of knowledge, leaving aside criticisms of his style of argument, is that he did not give a sociological explanation of the causes of the correspondence between conceptual systems and social organization. He did not consider causal explanations based on utility and interest, or as the result of people's interaction with their natural environment. (cf. Worsley, [14] and Lukes [9]). Where Durkheim and Mauss did offer a causal explanation, towards the end of *Primitive Classification,* it was by reference to psychological factors, to the effect that there are "sentimental affinities" between things, and that they are classified according to these affinities "for reasons of sentiment"[13] , p. 85.

The strongest form of Durkheim's argument was that which established structural correspondences, without resorting to psychological experiences to explain casuality. Durkheim and Mauss admitted that such states of collective emotion were not susceptible to sociological analysis:

> "Now emotion is naturally refractory to analysis, or at least lends itself uneasily to it, because it is too complex. Above all, when it has a collective origin it defies critical and rational examination" [13], p. 88.

It is worth noting that Claude Lévi-Strauss, who paid tribute to Durkheim as the source of many of his own ideas in developing structuralist analysis, claimed to have found a natural basis for explaining the ultimate structures of human culture without resorting to Durkheim's speculation about the emotional experience generated by social gatherings. Lévi-Strauss did this by developing another aspect of Durkheim's programme for sociology — the "forgotten part of the programme mapped out for it by Durkheim and Mauss":

"In his preface to the second edition of *The Rules of Sociological Method,* Durkheim defends himself against the charge of having unjustifiably separated the collective from the individual. He sees this separation as necessary but does not exclude the possiblity that in the future 'we will come to conceive the possibility of a completely formal psychology, which would be a sort of common ground of individual psychology and sociology . . .' 'What would be necessary' — Durkheim goes on — 'would be to seek, by the comparison of mythic themes, legends, popular traditions, and languages, in what way social representations call for each other or are mutually exclusive, merge with one another or remain distinct. . .'. He remarks, in closing, that this research pertains on the whole to the field of abstract logic"[15], pp. 24-5.

The main point of this structuralist approach, as developed by Lévi-Strauss, is that cultural phenomena such as kinship, myth, and totemism are analogous in their structure to language, and function as codes. Totemism was a language which enabled people to conceptualize thier social structure and the relationship of groups within it. Where Lévi-Strauss went beyond Durkheim was in his search for a natural basis for structuralism, and finding it in language, which had a physiological basis in nature. He followed the linguist Roman Jakobson in maintaining that language derived from a set of physiological constraints (concerning the mouth and larynx) and a set of mental principles which enabled speakers to encode and decode sounds (on the basis of binary opposition).

Both Mauss in his study of systems of reciprocity involved in giftgiving in simpler societies (*The Gift*)[16], and Lévi-Strauss in *Elementary Structures of Kinship* [17] (a title chosen to connect with Durkheim's *Elementary Forms*), developed that aspect of Durkheim's structuralism which disclosed the hidden, deeper structures, of which the people involved were not conscious. There were norms of which people were aware, in the sense of following obligatory rules; but these were often only the more obvious manifestations of more fundamental codes, which had to be followed for reasons of logic – one thing entailed another (or, was a *function* of another). The distinction is similar to that made in linguistics between the conscious norms – rules of grammar and semantics – and deeper structures of language of which we are not conscious. It is the deeper social structural principles or codes that provide the link between forms of social organization (i.e. ways of acting in relation to others) and collective representations (i.e. ways of thinking and believing). Whatever the deficiences in Durkheim's data and argument in the *Elementary Forms,* this case study of totemic religion and clan organization proved seminal for the development of sociological structuralist analysis.

3.7.5 Classification, Communication and Control

Perhaps the most successful efforts to show the relevance of Durkheim's findings for the study of social control in modern society have come from two British scholars, the social anthropologist, Mary Douglas, and the sociologist Basil Bernstein, both of whom could be described as neo-Durkheimians. Douglas, in one of her first works, began by applying Durkheim's ideas on the sacred and profane, and on ritual, to showing that our efforst at cleaning up, brushing away dirt, and putting things in their place, represent a ritualistic activity that functions to reaffirm the structured and categorical nature of social reality. The fact that dirt could be defined as "matter out of place" indicated the existence of an underlying category system or order of things that varied from society to society, and over time. The symbols of purity and impurity, particularly those that related to relations between categories and groups of people, such as between castes in India and between the sexes in many societies, mirrored designs of social hierarchy. Douglas also made clear the common relevance of Durkheim's ideas for her work and for Bernstein's, which used Durkheim's distinction between groups with "mechanical solidarity" and those with "organic solidarity" to show that these integrative characteristics corresponded with the use of different speech codes. Groups with mechanical solidarity tended to have a "restricted" speech code (i.e. a narrower range of syntactic alternatives, with the alternatives more rigidly organized, and heavy dependence on social context), whereas groups with organic solidarity tend to have a more "elaborated" speech code (i.e. wider range of syntactic alternatives, more flexibly organized, less dependent on social context, more abstract, etc.). Douglas suggested that ritual was a form of communication with a restricted code, and that different types of communication corresponded to different types of social control. In Bernstein's case he showed that the different linguistic codes and types of social control corresponded to different social classes and their cultures, as illustrated by the disadvantaged situation of working class children whose restricted speech code was a handicap in schools where success depended on conforming to an elaborated speech code.

The result of these cross-fertilizations deriving from Durkheim's seminal work on religion has been to confirm his contention that fundamental insights into the relations between the individual and social groups could be gained from a comparative approach which began by analysing social structures and cultures in their most rudimentary form. The task of Durkheim's sociological successors has been to develop and critically adapt his ideas for the purpose of analysing the structures and cultures of modern complex societies. (cf. Douglas, [2, 3], Bernstein, [18]).

REFERENCES

[1] Emile Durkheim, *The Elementary Forms of the Religious Life,* trs. J. W. Swain, New York, Free Press, paperback edn. 1965.

[2] Mary Douglas, *Purity and Danger,* London, Routledge & Kegan Paul, 1966.

[3] Mary Douglas, *Natural Symbols,* London, Barrie & Rockliff, 1970, and Pelican Books edn. 1973.

[4] Robert N. Bellah, "Civil Religion in America", *Daedalus,* 96, (Winter, 1967), pp. 1-21.

[5] Peter L. Berger, & Thomas Luckmann, *The Social Construction of Reality,* London, Penguin, 1967.

[6] Peter L. Berger, *The Social Reality of Religion,* London, Faber 1969, published as *The Sacred Canaopy,* New York, Doubleday, 1967.

[7] Will Herberg, *Protestant — Catholic — Jew,* New York, Doubleday, 1960.

[8] E. E. Evans-Pritchard, *Theories of Primitive Religion,* Oxford, Clarendon Press, 1965.

[9] Steven Lukes, *Emile Durkheim,* London, Allen Lane, 1973, Peregrine paperback edn. 1975.

[10] Bernard Lacroix, *"The Elementary Forms of Religious Life* as a Reflection on Power (*Objet Pouvoir)*", in *Critique of Anthropology,* 4, 13-14, 1979, pp. 87-103.

[11] Guy Swanson, *The Birth of the Gods; The Origin of Primitive Beliefs,* Ann Arbor, Michigan, University of Michigan Press, 1960.

[12] Kai Erikson, *Wayward Puritans,* New York, Wiley, 1966.

[13] Emile Durkheim & Marcel Mauss, *Primitive Classification,* trs. Rodney Needham, London, Cohen & West, and Chicago, University of Chicago Press, 1963.

[14] Peter Worsley, "E. Durkheim's Theory of Knowledge", in *Sociological Review,* n.s. **4,** 1, 1956, pp. 47-62.

[15] Claude Lévi-Strauss, *Structural Anthropology* vol. 2, New York, Basic Books, 1976.

[16] Marcel Mauss, *The Gift,* trs. I. Cunnison, London & New York, Free Press, 1954.

[17] Claude Lévi-Strauss, *The Elementary Structures of Kinship,* trs. R. Needham, London, 1969.

[18] Basil Bernstein, *Class, Codes and Control,* 3 vols., London, Routledge & Kegan Paul, 1971-5.

[19] Edward Shils and Michael Young, "The meaning of the coronation," *Sociological Review,* vol. 1, no. 2, 1953, pp. 63-82.

[20] Norman Birnbaum, "Monarchs and sociologists: a reply to Professor Shils and Mr Young," *Sociological Review,* vol. 3, no. 1, 1955, pp. 5-23.

[21] Nicholas Abercrombie, Stephen Hill and Bryan S. Turner, *The Dominant Ideology Thesis,* London, Allen & Unwin, 1980.

3.8 POLITICS

3.8.1 Outline and evaluation

Durkheim's most important work on politics was not published until thirty-three years after his death, and even then it was as the result of the efforts of a Turkish disciple and as a publication of the University of Istanbul. Based on Durkheim's lecture notes, the book had the title: *Lecons de sociologie: physique des meurs et du droit* (1950). It was published in an English translation in 1957 with the title *Professional Ethics and Civic Morals* [1]. Not surprisingly, in view of this history, the most influential early accounts in English of Durkheim's sociology were written without reference to this work (e.g. Alpert [2], Parsons [3]), and underplayed the political content of his thought. Parsons, especially, was responsible for promoting the idea that Durkheim's sociology developed towards a more "idealist" position in his later work, with shared values and religion becoming the focus in place of the topic of changing forms of social organization featured in *The Division of Labour in Society.* It is only in recent years that there has been a reassessment of the extent to which Durkheim's sociology was concerned with political problems and the nature of the modern state (cf. Giddens [4]).

In addition to this tendency of American commentators to assimilate Durkheim's thought into a contemporary "functionist" or "voluntarist" approach, he has also suffered misrepresentation from teachers of sociology who found it convenient to contrast different approaches by identifying them with specific individuals. Consequently, Durkheim was identified with an approach preoccupied with "order" and "stability", in contrast to Marx, who could be protrayed as concerned with "conflict" and "change".

This does not do justice to Durkheim's position. A better acquaintance with his writings on politics in works such as *Professional Ethics and Civic Morals, Socialism* [5], and in his articles, reviews, and correspondence, has led to a greater appreciation of his concern about the need for social change in order to fulfil the ideals of the French Revolution – liberty, equality, and fraternity. Unlike Marx, however, he did not believe that fundemantal and lasting changes of a progressive kind could be brought about by a political revolution based on class conflict. Drawing on the experience of France since the 1789 Revolution, he concluded that political revolutions tended to lead to bureaucratic domination: "It is among the most revolutionary people that bureaucratic routine is often most powerful"; in such societies "superficial mobility disguises the most monotonous uniformity" [6]. In fact his position was not dissimilar from that of Marx on the prospects for a successful revolution in a society, such as Russia, where social and political organization had not evolved to a point where it could sustain revolutionary changes. In Durkheim's view, the problem in France was that the underlying social changes, of which the Revolution of 1789 and the revolutionary movements of 1848 and 1870–71 were only a symptom, had not yet been accommodated within the structure of modern France. The task of sociology was to show the long-term evolutionary character of the changes that had brought about industrialization (the division of labour) and which had still to come to fruition. This was the analytical task taken up in the first book, *The Division of Labour in Society*, and continued in *Professional Ethics and Civic Morals*.

The differentiation of institutions and functions entailed in the division of labour produced a situation marked by greatly increased individualism. This could be a positive development or it could have pathological results, depending on the type of individualism that prevailed. As it had developed in France and other capitalist societies it had taken on pathological characteristics – egoism rathen than moral individualism threatened to predominate. It was each man for himself, rather than each for every other. Competition and conflict to satisfy individual, unrestrained appetites reigned in place of cooperation to promote the common good. Freedom of contract in this situation of inequality simply meant that the strong exploited the weak. The situation could only be changed if the state took a more positive role in securing the conditions under which individuals could develop their potentialities, involving equality of opportunity and a drastic reduction in the inequalities perpetuated through the inheritance of wealth. A crucial reform would be the development of intermediate institutions between the individual and the state, so as to cohere the opinions of individuals and communicate them to the state, and to channel the state's leadership down to the grassroots; such institutions would also act as a buffer between the individual and the state, and balance the power of the state. Because of the importance of the economic sphere in industrial societies, the key intermediate institution would be one that combined economic and moral functions — these should be occupational associations, analogous to the ancient guilds or corporations.

This analysis, as developed in *Professional Ethics and Civic Morals*, can be seen to have been a direct continuation of that begun in the *Division of Labour*. Contrary to the impression given by some sociological critics, Durkheim's sociology was not a conservative hankering after a return to the stability of the past, nor was it a manifestation of an authoritarian urge to subjugate the individual to society.

His thought was not part of the stream that flowed from the "counter-reaction" against the French Revolution. Far from wishing to defend "order" against change, his sociological analysis had the objective of helping society to see what had to be done to achieve change. There could be no going back to the mechanical solidarity of simpler societies, in which the individual was subordinated to the collective conscience, based on uniformity. There was still a "sacred" quality in society, and it attached to social ideals; in the modern era they were ideals concerning respect for the dignity and worth of the individual. These ideals of moral individualism could only be fulfilled if society was organized in such a way as to enable the individual to govern himself, that is to control the appetites and be free to realize his potential and to assist others to do the same. Solidary groups and group ethics were required.

3.8.2 Professional Ethics and Civic Morals

This work, *Professional Ethics and Civic Morals*, makes it clear that Durkheim was not neglectful of issues of class conflict, as some critics have alleged. In a sense it was his major concern. But he regarded it as a symptom of the fact that the economy was not subject to agreed moral discipline. Consequently it was not enough simply to reform the economy in a once-and-for-all measure; it needed to be kept in constant regulation so that it served moral ends:

> "There has been talk, and not without reason, of societies becoming mainly industrial. A form of activity that promises to occupy such a place in society taken as a whole cannot be exempt from all precise moral regulation, without a state of anarchy ensuing. The forces thus released can have no guidance for their normal development, since there is nothing to point out where a halt should be called. There is a head-on clash when the moves of rivals conflict as they attempt to encroach on another's field or to beat him down or drive him out. Certainly the stronger succeed in crushing the not so strong or at any rate in reducing them to a state of subjection. But since this subjection is only a *de facto* condition sanctioned by no kind of morals, it is accepted only under duress until the longed-for day of revenge. Peace treaties signed in this fashion are always provisional, forms of truce that do not mean peace to men's minds. This is how these ever-recurring conflicts arise between the different factions of the economic structure. If we put forward this anarchic competition as an ideal we should adhere to — one that should even be put into practice more radically than it is today — then we should be confusing sickness with a condition of good health. On the other hand, we should not get away from this simply by modifying once and for all the lay-out of economic life; for whatever we contrive, whatever new arrangements be introduced, it will not become other than it is or change its nature. By its very nature, it cannot be self-sufficing. A state of order or peace among men cannot follow of itself from any entirely material causes, from any blind mechanism, however scientific it may be. It is a moral task." [1], pp. 11-12.

It can be seen that he was critical of advocates of free enterprise and *laissez-faire* economic policies, and of theories of scientific socialism in so far as they were predominantly economic theories. In his opinion, the amoral and immoral aspects of the economic system would only be cured if the people in each occupation and industry regulated their own activities on the basis of their own systems of ethics:

> "For in this order of social functions there is need for professional ethics to be established, nearer the concrete, closer to the facts, with a wider scope than anything existing today. There should be rules telling each of the workers his rights and duties, not vaguely in general terms but in precise detail, having in view the most

ordinary day-to-day occurrences. All these various interrelations cannot remain for ever in a state of fluctuating balance. A system of ethics, however, is not to be improvised. It is the task of the very group to which they are to apply. When they fail it is because the cohesion of the group is at fault, because as a group its existence is too shadowy and the rudimentary state of its ethics goes to show its lack of integration. Therefore, the true cure for the evil is to give the professional groups in the economic order a stability they so far do not possess. While the craft union or corporate body is nowadays only a collection of individuals who have no lasting ties one with another, it must become or return to being a well-defined and organized association." [1], pp. 12–13.

He saw no reason why membership of such occupational groups should not be compulsory, and could not understand objections to the principle of the closed-shop:

..."it is beyond me to understand the scruples that some feel in this case against any suggestion of compulsion. Every citizen nowadays is obliged to be attached to a *commune* (parish). Why then should the same principle not apply to the profession or calling?" [1], p. 39.

Durkheim believed the state could not regulate the various functions of the economy, except at a very general, coordination and planning level; regulation had to be pluralistic and decentralized, in the hands of the people actually involved in production. Furthermore, this pluralistic, self-regulation of producer groups was a more basic prerequisite change than a single socialist measure such as changing the ownership of the means of production. Simply changing the ownership, e.g. nationaliza-tion, would still leave unresolved the question of regulation, and whether it was to be imposed from above or generated by the people affected by it:

"This is why I believe that no reform has greater urgency. I will not say it would achieve everything, but it is the preliminary condition that makes all the others possible. Let us suppose that by a miracle the whole system of property is entirely transformed overnight, and that on the collectivist formula the means of production are taken out of the hands of individuals and made over absolutely to collec-tive ownership. All the problems around us that we are debating today will still persist in their entirety. There will always be an economic mechanism and various agencies to combine in making it work. The rights and obligations of these various agencies therefore have to be determined, and in the different branches of industry at that. So a corpus of rules has to be laid down, fixing the stint of work, the pay of the members of staff, and their obligations to one another, towards the community, and so on. This means, then, that we should still be faced with a blank page to work on. Supposing the means — the machinery of labour — had been taken out of these hands or those and placed in others, we should still not know how the machinery worked or what the economic life should be, nor what to do in the face of this change in conditions. The state of anarchy would still persist; for, let me repeat, this state of anarchy comes about not from this machinery being in these hands and not in those, but because the activity deriving from it is not regulated. And it will not be regulated, nor its moral standard raised, by any witchcraft. This control by rule and raising of moral standards can be established neither by the scientist in his study nor by the statesman; it has to be the task of the groups concerned. Since these groups do not exist at the present time it is of the utmost urgency that they be created. The other problems can only be usefully tackled after that." [1], p. 31.

Durkheim had no scruple about abolishing private property ownership, although he thought it would be difficult to do it at a stroke; public opinion would demand that a parent should be able to pass on at least a modest amount of property to children. However, the main point of his discussion of property was to show that there was nothing sacred about property ownership in modern society. There was no immutable principle that could determine property rights and fair contract, because these were ideas relative to the morals and opinion of society in each period and type of society. He believed the trend of social evolution was towards a morality that favoured equality of opportunity for each individual. Property inheritance was archaic because it derived from a prior period when the family was the social unit to which property was attached, because the original form of property was land, which was immovable. Now, inherited wealth was the main source of class divisions and produced a basic polarization between two classes (a doctrine reminiscent of Marx):

"Now inheritance as an institution results in men being born either rich or poor; that is to say, there are two main classes in society, linked by all sorts of intermediate classes: the one which in order to live has to make its services acceptable to the other at whatever the cost; the other class which can do without these services, because it can call on certain resources, which may, however, not be equal to the services rendered by those who have them to offer. Therefore as long as such sharp class differences exist in society, fairly effective palliatives may lessen the injustice of contracts; but in principle, the system operates in conditions which do not allow of justice. It is not only to cover certain particular points that 'lion's share' contracts can be entered into, but the contract represents the 'lion's share' system as far as any relations of the two classes are concerned. It is the general lines on which the services of those not favoured by fortune are assessed that seems unjust, because the conditions stand in the way of their being reckoned at their true social value. The inherited fortune loads the scales and upsets the balance. It is in opposition to this inequitable assessment and to the whole state of society that allows it to happen, that we get the growing revolt of men's conscience. It is true that over the centuries, the injustice could be accepted without revolt because the demand for equality was less. Today, however, it conflicts only too obviously with the attitude which is found underlying our morality" [1], pp. 213-214.

The solution, he maintained, was to abolish the inheritance of property (p. 216). After all, it was no longer possible to bequeath titles and offices to one's descendants; "Why should property be any more transferable?" (p. 216). However, he recognized that people in general might put up a lively resistance if it was proposed to prevent them leaving any possessions to their family, because it would offend certain deeply-rooted family customs. Some inheritance might survive in weakened form: "We might, for instance, imagine that every head of a family would have the right to leave to his children specified portions of the heritage" (p. 217). The surplus wealth would not go to the state, which was "already so blundering and wasteful" and "too far removed from things and individuals to be able to carry out the tasks so vast and so complex with any competence". There would have to be secondary groups, more limited in range and closer to the facts in detail, to be able to fulfil this function. "We could hardly choose any better suited to the task than the professional groups" (p. 218). However, he seemed to envisage the persistence of a distinct strata of "employers" and the need for their separate representation, at least for some industries.

The State

Durkheim's theory of politics and the state, as set out in *Professional Ethics and Civic Morals*, entailed a perception of a fundamental opposition and analytical distinction between the governed and the governors: "An essential element that enters into the notion of any political group is the opposition between the governing and the governed, between authority and those subject to it" (p. 42). However, authority relations also existed in institutions other than the state, for example in the patriarchal family, so he added one further characteristic of political society or the state. He rejected territory as a defining characteristic, despite its inclusion in many other theories of the state, because the family had also had its own territory, and nomadic societies had elaborate structures but no territory. The defining characteristic was sovereignty over secondary groups:

> "We should then define the political society as one formed by the coming together of a rather large number of secondary social groups, subject to the same one authority, which is not itself subject to any other superior authority duly constituted"[1], p. 45.

One slight complication was presented by federal states, in which each individual state was autonomous to a certain degree. Consequently, said Durkheim, we should not make any hard-and-fast distinction, but see political societies as more or less state formations depending on the degree to which they had a sovereign independence as opposed to being subordinate to a superior organ (p. 47). He admitted that the use of the terms "political society" and "state" were not always distinguished, even in his own writings. However, an effort should be made to maintain a distinction between the state proper, and its associated institutions.

Some theorists of the state blur the distinction between it and associated institutions, such as the military, the Church, education, etc., on the grounds that they are part of the state because they incorporate the ideology of the ruling class (thus, Althusser [7] refers to them as "Ideological State Apparatuses"). Durkheim emphasized the relative autonomy of the state and its distinctive functions. By the state he meant mainly the policy-making level of government, and although he noted that it could come under pressure from ideologies and forces of opinion stemming from other sectors of society, he maintained that the state was the originating source of a particular type of ideology or consciousness. Its decisions might be affected by ideological forces emanating from outside itself, but its decisions

"... above all express the particular milieu where it has its origin. It often happens, too, that there may even be discord between this milieu and the nation as a whole, and that decisions taken by the government or parliamentary vote may be valid for the whole community and yet do not square with the state of social opinion. So we may say that there is a collective psychic life, but this life is not diffused throughout the entire social body: although collective, it is localized in a specific organ. And this localization does not come about simply through concentration on a given point of a life having its origins outside this point. It is in part at this very point that it has its beginning. When the state takes thought and makes a decision, we must not say that it is the society that thinks and decides through the state, but that the state thinks and decides for it" [1], p. 49.

Durkheim defined the state in terms of its function:

"It is a group of officials *sui generis*, within which representations and acts of volition involving the collectivity are worked out, although they are not the product of the collectivity. ... To sum up, we can therefore say that the state is a special organ whose responsibility it is to work out certain representations which hold good for the collectivity. These representations are distinguished from other collective representations by their higher degree of consciousness and reflection" [1], pp. 49-50.

Thus the state was the organ of social thought and its supreme decision-maker. He distinguished the state proper from the executive which carries out the decisions. The state proper originated the decisions and the thinking about them – it was like the central nervous system, and the executive was similar to the muscular system.

He had a positive view of the state, unlike some conservatives, and he did not think the growth in the state's activities need be at the expense of the individual, in contrast to the view of Herbert Spencer. The state could be liberating for the individual. His only objection to theories which took as their object the protection and development of the rights and capacities of the individual was that they did not see the need to order the state in such a way as to make these aspirations feasible and durable [1], p. 60. Durkheim's positive view of the state also required that nation states should turn away from old tendencies to imperialist expansion and rivalry. But in turning inwards they should not concentrate solely on economic development – the production of more goods was not a sufficient goal. The aim of the state should be to promote social justice and the full development of all citizens:

> "The planning of the social milieu so that the individual may realize himself more fully, and the management of the collective apparatus in a way that will bear less hard on the individual; an assured and amicable exchange of goods and services and the cooperation of all men of good will towards an ideal they share without any conflict; in these, surely, we have enough to keep public activity fully employed" [1], p. 71.

In turning away from war and international conflict, and away from militarism, the society should not become "a vast digestive apparatus":

> "It is not merely a matter of increasing the exchanges of goods and services, but of seeing that they are done by rules that are more just; it is not simply that everyone should have access to rich supplies of food and drink. Rather, it is that each one should be treated as he deserves, each be freed from an unjust and humiliating tutelage, and that, in holding to his fellows and his group, a man should not sacrifice his individuality. And the agency on which this special responsibility lies is the state" [1], pp. 71-2.

One final subject that Durkheim discussed was that of national patriotism versus world patriotism, or internationalism. He believed that a world state was too far in the future to enter current reckoning, and he did not think a European Community (a confederation of European states) would advance matters very much:

> "A confederation of European States, for instance, is advanced, but vainly, as a half-way course to achieving societies on a bigger scale than those we know today. This greater confederation, again, would be like an individual state, having its own identity and its own interests and features. It would not be humanity" [1], p. 74.

He considered it unfortunate that patriotism seemed to manifest itself in conflicts and wars with outside entities. A better kind of patriotism would be one which was internally oriented:

> "As long as there are states, so there will be national pride, and nothing can be more warranted. But societies can have their pride, not in being the greatest or the wealthiest, but in being the most just,

the best organized and in possessing the best moral constitution"
[1], p.75.

Ever the realist, he concluded, "To be sure, we have not yet reached the
point when this kind of patriotism could prevail without dissent, if
indeed such a time could ever come". Clearly he was no starry-eyed
optimist, as his critics have sometimes suggested. He walked the difficult
and seldom intellectually glamorous road of patient analysis and
constructive reform.

Conclusions

Durkheim's involvement with practical politics was slight. He feared it
would distract him and his collaborators on L'Anneé sociologique from
their task of building up scientific sociology, especially as earlier
sociologists such as Comte and Saint-Simon had brought sociology into
disrepute among serious scholars by substituting preaching for scientific
analysis. There was a further scruple that prevented Durkheim from
injecting a stronger partisan element into his sociology, and that was his
belief that the teacher should not exploit his professional position to
make political propaganda. (In this he resembled Max Weber, his German
contemporary.)

The closest he came to political involvement, apart from the Dreyfus
Affair, was with the solidarist movement. He spoke at the international
conference on solidarism, held as part of the Exposition Universelle of
1900, and he was widely quoted in solidarist literature. However, this
was probably the full extent of his participation, and his own position
on solidarity was nearer to that of those nineteenth-century leftist and
reformist movements for whom it equated with basic social reform,
rather than the diluted version of the amorphous movement in the Third
Republic. (cf. La Capra [8], p.73; a contrasting view is given in Hayward
[9]; a discussion of the impact of Durkheim's ideas on Georges Sorel,
and on syndicalism and fascism, is provided by Roberts [10]).

The political implications of Durkheim's sociology have been
likened to the British tradition of non-Marxist, socialist critique of
capitalism, a prominent exponent of which was R. H. Tawney (1880-
1962). Like Tawney, Durkheim looked for a way of transcending class
divisions through social reform, the establishment of a kind of guild
socialism based on ethical community with a vision of social justice,
and where power would be responsibly exercised because it would be
grounded in equality of respect for other individuals. (cf. Eldridge [11],
Tawney [12].) And, like Tawney, Durkheim believed that a society based
on competition, exploitation, and rivalry (i.e. contemporary capitalism)
could not be consistent with a fraternal society of equals.

Where Durkheim differed from what he took to be the Marxist view of exploitation, was that he did not think the evils of capitalism derived solely from exploitation of one class by another, but also from the exploitation of man's selfish instincts, giving rise to insatiable consumerism and striving for wealth. Consumerism can exist even after the ownership of the means of production has been socialized. Durkheim did not have any attachment to the system of private ownership of property — there was nothing sacred about it, and it was a remnant of a territorially-based family ownership system. The exploitations that Durkheim thought were more difficult to abolish, and therefore more important to grapple with, were the exploitations of wealth-seeking, consumerism, and bureaucratic domination. (One of his criticisms of socialist doctrines was that they focused on economic issues to the detriment of any consideration of the sources and solutions of these other pathological tendencies.)

His objection to most economic doctrines of his day was that they studied economic functions as if they were an end in themselves, rather than a means to an end:

"Society has no justification if it does not bring a little peace to men — peace in their hearts and peace in their mutual intercourse. If, then, industry can be productive only by disturbing their peace and unleashing warfare, it is not worth the cost" [1], p. 16.

3.8.3 Socialism

Le Socialisme was also published posthumously (in 1928, English translation 1958 [5]). It was based on the first part of a course of lectures on the history of socialism that Durkheim delivered at Bordeaux, from 1895 to 1896. His interest in socialism dated from his time at the Ecole Normale Superieure, his contacts with the so-called "Socialists of the chair" in Germany, and his original conception for a doctoral thesis on "The relationship of individualism and socialism". An additional reason for giving this course of lectures was that many of his brightest students were converted to socialism, and even formed a study circle to examine Marx's Capital. He saw the need for subjecting this movement and its ideas to sociological analysis in terms of a sociology of knowledge approach. He treated it as an ideology, which could be related to the social structures and conditions which had determined its existence and form.

The book contains only the first part of the projected history: Definition, Beginnings of socialism, and Saint-Simon. Later sections were to cover Proudhon, Lasalle, Marx, and German socialism; but

"It is indisputable that it has thus rendered social science more services perhaps than it has received from it. For, it has aroused reflection, it has stimulated scientific activity, it has instigated research, posed problems, so that in more than one way its history blends with the very history of sociology" [5], p. 40.

Socialism had tried to pass off as science a variety of opinions and prognostications concerning all aspects of social order, even in areas where research was still in its infancy. The basis for prediction had not been established: "Socialism has not taken the time; perhaps one could even say, it did not have the time" [5], p. 40. This charge applied even to the work of Marx:

"The only attitude that science permits in the face of these problems is reservation and circumspection, and socialism can hardly maintain this without lying to itself. And, in fact, socialism has not maintained this attitude. Not even the strongest work — the most systematic, the richest in ideas — that this school has produced: Marx's *Capital*. What statistical data, what historical comparisons, what studies would be indispensable to solve any one of the innumerable questions that are dealt with there! ... Socialism is not a science, a sociology in miniature — it is a cry of grief, sometimes of anger, uttered by men who feel most keenly our collective malaise. Socialism is to the facts which produce it what the groans of a sick man are to the illness with which he is afflicted, to the needs that torment him. But what would one say of a doctor who accepted the replies or desires of his patient as scientific truths? Moreover, the theories ordinarily offered in opposition to socialism are no different in nature and they no more merit the title we refuse the latter. When economists call for *laissez-faire,* demanding that the influence of the state be reduced to nothing, that competition be freed of every restraint, they are not basing their claims on laws scientifically developed. The social sciences are still much too young to be able to serve as bases for practical doctrines, which are so vast and of such breadth" [5], pp. 40-41.

It is not difficult to see why Durkheim felt that his first priority was to devote himself to *L'Année sociologique* and the task of building up sociology. But because he avoided involvement in political struggles he failed to develop an appreciation of the strength of the class interests that frustrated political development along the lines he had envisaged. The most serious criticism of his political sociology is that it did not face up to the proloms of changing the existing division of labour based on opposing class interests, and perpetuated by state institutions which were part of the existing relations of class domination and subordination.

REFERENCES

[1] Émile Durkheim, *Professional Ethics and Civic Morals*, trs. by C. Brookfield, London, Routledge & Keegan Paul, 1957.

[2] Harry Alpert, *Émile Durkheim and His Sociology*, New York, Columbia University Press, 1939.

[3] Talcott Parsons, *The Structure of Social Action*, New York, McGraw-Hill, 1937.

[4] Anthony Giddens, "Durkhein's Political Sociology", *Sociological Review*, 19, 4, 1971, pp. 477-519.

[5] Émile Durkheim, *Socialism*, trs. by C. Sattler, introductions by M. Mauss and A. Gouldner, New York, Collier Books, 1962, and London, Collier-Macmillan paperback edn.; first published in English as *Socialism and Saint-Simon*, Antioch Press, 1958.

[6] Émile Durkheim, *Moral Education*, trs. by E. K. Wilson and H. Schnurer, New York, Free Press, and London, Collier-Macmillan, 1961.

[7] Louis Althusser, "Ideology and Ideological State Apparatuses" in his *Lenin and Philosophy and Other Essays*, London, New Left Books, 1971.

[8] Dominick La Capra, *Émile Durkheim: Sociologist and Philosopher*, Ithaca, Cornell University Press, 1972.

[9] J. E. S. Hayward, "Solidarity: The Social History of an Idea in Nineteenth Century France", *International Review of Social History*, n.s. IV, 1972, pp. 261-284.

[10] David D. Roberts, *The Syndicalist Tradition and Italian Fascism*, Chapel Hill, N-C., University of North Carolina Press, 1979.

[11] John Eldridge, *Recent British Sociology*, London, Macmillan, 1980.

[12] R. H. Tawney, *The Acquisitive Society*, London, Bell, 1921.

3.9 EDUCATION
3.9.1 Morals and Education

Both at Bordeaux and Paris, Durkheim's university appointments were to lecture primarily on education to trainee school teachers, with sociology as a subsidiary responsibility (almost a case of smuggling in sociology by the back door to avoid the entrenched opposition). Two of the most important sets of lectures on education were published shortly after his death: *Education and Sociology* (1922, English translation 1956 [1]) and *Moral Education* (1925, English trs. 1961 [2]). The third, *The Evolution of Educational Thought,* was published in 1938 and not translated into English until 1977 [3]; it is perhaps the most neglected of his works, despite the fact that it is an important demonstration of his structural sociology in a historical mode, and it is vital for understanding his conception of ideology. It is significant methodologically because it combines historical and sociological analysis in a subtle way, and so serves to correct the impression that *Suicide* was the work most representative of his sociological method. Taken along with *Professional Ethics and Civic Morals* it dispels the mistaken view that his sociology was inherently conservative in its political implications.

Central to his teaching on educational theory and practice was the subject of morals, which he interpreted in a very broad sense to refer to rules of various sorts. He applied his method of structural analysis to show that morals and educational ideas and practices were socially determined. Education was "the means by which society perpetually re-creates the conditions of its very existence" and it involved "a systematic socialization of the young generation"[1], pp. 123-124. Educational reform was a high priority of the Third Republic, which required the formulation and inculation of an appropriate secular morality to replace that of the Church. Durkheim's first task was to show that there was nothing absolute about systems of morals, because they were socially relative, and, therefore, the formulation of an appropriate morality for modern society could only proceed after the lessons had been learned about how morality had functioned in relation to previous social structures.

All moral behaviour shared a common characteristic: it was behaviour that conformed to pre-existing rules. "Morality consists of a system of rules of action that predetermine conduct"[2], p. 24. It laid down limits beyond which individual behaviour could not deviate without bringing sanctions into play. It was not a question of individuals constantly making decisions as to how to behave by consulting some general principle. A moral system was internalized and shaped behaviour: it was "a totality of definite rules; it is like so many molds with limiting boundaries, into which we pour our behaviour" (ibid). The regularity that is characteristic of moral behaviour was not simply the result of habit; "it is a way of acting that we do not feel free to alter according to taste". (ibid, p. 28). An added characteristic was the sense of authority: "By authority we must understand that influence which imposes upon us all the moral power that we acknowledge as superior to us." (ibid, p. 29). The regularity and authority of rules were bound together by the spirit of discipline: "Discipline in effect regularizes conduct. It implies repetitive behaviour under determinate conditions." (ibid, p. 31). The second characteristic element related to the content of morality, which Durkheim described as "attachment to social groups". To act morally was to act in terms of the collective interest: "Man acts morally only when he works towards goals superior to, or beyond, individual goals." (ibid, p. 69). Self-interest and the sum of self-interests could only be amoral, which was represented in the egoistic individualism that characterised contemporary capitalist society. This was quite different from "moral individualism", which required of moral behaviour an extra characteristic in modern society — that of "autonomy". It was not enought to act morally out of respect for authority or commitment to a group; moral action had to be rational, based on as complete an awareness as possible of the reasons for our conduct.

Moral education had to enable the child to carry out a symbolic explanation of the rule itself, its cause and reasons for being. (ibid, p. 120). Sociology, allied with history, could help the teacher to develop this kind of ability in children. The course summarized in *The Evolution of Educational Thought* [3] aimed to develop just such an appreciation of the social factors that had caused moral and educational ideas to take certain forms in specific periods.

Finally, Durkheim has been criticized for his stress on education's function of serving to reproduce society. It is alleged that this represents a conservative stress on stability and a neglect of education as an instrument of social change. In fact, Durkheim made it clear that he did not think teachers should rest content with reproducing society as it had existed; a society without conflict and change would be a stagnant and medicore society:

"A society in which there is pacific commerce between its members, in which there is no conflict of any sort, but which has nothing more than that, would have a rather medicore qualtiy. Society must, in addition, have before it an ideal toward which it reaches. . . . It must go on to new conquests; it is necessary that the teacher prepare the children who are in his trust for these necessary advances. He must be on his guard against transmitting the moral gospel of our elders as a sort of closed book. On the contrary, he must excite in them a desire to add a few lines of their own, and give them the tools to satisfy this legitimate ambition"[3], pp. 13-4.

However, Durkheim remained extremely cautious about the

prospects for making radical social changes through education alone. As we have noted earlier, in discussing the prospects for education acting as a cure for suicide and other social ills, he warned that it was a mistake to ascribe to education a power it lacked; it tended to reproduce society rather than to change it. It was for this reason that he took a sceptical view of the possibilities for counteracting the bad effects of the division of labour into minute tasks by giving workers a general education of a more literary kind. As he put it: "No doubt, it is good for the worker to be interested in art, literature, etc., but it is none the less bad that he should be treated as a machine all day" [2], p. 372.

One of the main criticisms of Durkheim's sociology has been to the effect that he did not see that ideology, as represented by moral and education doctrines and practices, could be biased and systematically work in favour of the interests of some classes against those of others. Added to this is the charge that he was blind to education's role in restricting the life-chances of some classes. (cf. Lukes [4], p. 133.) However, these charges are completely refuted by his historical analyses of the relations between social classes and educational ideas and practices, as set out in *The Evolution of Educational Thought*. A good example is provided by his analysis of the educational changes brought about by the Renaissance. He explained these as the result of economic factors and changes in the position of certain classes, particularly the newly-wealthy "leisured class". His argument was that a growth in wealth and consumption led to an increasing emulation of aristocratic life-styles by the aspiring middle class, and a change in educational ideas. The educational ideas of Humanism, as exemplified by Erasmus, were directed towards refinement of cultural tastes to fit the "leisured class" for polite society. And, Durkheim added, this was at the cost of the total neglect of the educational needs of the masses:

"Thus the educational ideas of the Humanists were not the result of simple accidents; they derived rather from a fact whose influence on the moral history of our country it is difficult to exaggerate; I refer to the establishment of polite society. ... The object of education as Erasmus conceived it was to prepare men for this special and restricted society. Here too we can see the essential character and at the same time the radical flaw of this educational theory. It is essentially aristocratic in nature. The kind of society which it seeks to fashion is always centred around a court, and its members are always drawn from the ranks of the aristocracy or at least from the leisured classes.

Neither Erasmus nor Vivès had any awareness that beyond this small world, which for all its brilliance was very limited, there were vast masses who should not have been neglected, and for whom education should have raised their intellectual and moral standards and improved their material condition. ... For the majority the supreme need is survival; and what is needed in order to survive is not the art of subtle speech, it is the art of sound thinking so that one knows how to act. In order to struggle effectively in the world of persons and the world of things, more substantial weapons are needed than those glittering decorations with which the Humanist educationalists were concerned to adorn the mind to the exclusion of everything else" [3], pp. 205-206.

There is no better example of Durkheim's structural mode of analysis than that contained in his discussion of the ideology of Humanism. In addition to examining the morphological structural facts that had determined it, he also examined the confluence of collective representations that structured the ideology itself:

"In fact 'man', as Humanist teachers portrayed and continue to portray him, was no more than the product of a synthesis between Christian, Roman, and Greek ideals; and it was these three ideals which were used to mould him, because it was these three ideals which had moulded the consciousness of those who expounded him. ... There is consequently no justification whatsoever for presenting it as the only ideal conception of man, the only one which expresses the true nature of man; it stands, on the contrary, in very definite causal relationship to a particular time and a particular place" [3], pp. 326-327.

The teacher, drawing on sociology and history, could help the child to see these social determinants of ideology and so enable the child to make rational judgements based on an enlightened consciousness. And once the variability of human nature became understood in the light of an understanding of its determination by social structural factors, then the "commonsense" or "natural" claims of the ideology would be exposed as false, and the possibilities for change would be revealed.

CONCLUSION

Durkheim's view of the mission of sociology was that it should become a scientific discipline, using structural analysis to reveal how social being determines consciousness, and that the ensuing enlightened consciousness should enable us to make judicious changes that would last. Neither conservative nor revolutionary, he believed that lasting change could only be brought about by painstaking analysis and laborious effort. He was convinced that sociological analysis could have profound effects by changing people's consciousness. For example, its revelation of the structural determinants of human nature "differs dramatically from that implied in and propagated by the traditional Humanist education" and "the value of seeing man this way is not of a purely theoretical kind; for, as we should expect, our conception of man is also capable of affecting our conduct" [3], pp. 328-9. The result of developing a sociological consciousness would be to open up the existing conception of human nature, which was "narrowly and rigidly circumscribed" and "essentially hostile to any innovation of real significance"; consequently "any reform which depends on a relatively radical modification of human desires most easily strikes us as a dangerous and impracticable utopianism" (ibid). The sociologically informed consciousness or imagination could open up mental horizons and teach us that "we ought to become very suspicious of claims to be able to restrict the possible scope of evolution in the future" (ibid).

Durkheim had little of Marx's romantic vision of the possibilities for revolutionary change. But he was remarkably open-minded and cautiously optimistic. His dedication to the vocation of sociologist was at the same time a dedication to analysing the structural determinants of social change:

"What history teaches us is that man does not change arbitrarily; he does not transform himself at will on hearing the voices of inspired prophets. The reason is that all change, in colliding with the inherited institutions of the past, is inevitably hard and laborious; consequently it only takes place in response to the demands of necessity. For change to be brought about it is not enough that it should be seen as desirable; it must be the product of changes within the whole network of diverse causal relationships which determine the situation of man" [3], pp. 329-30.

REFERENCES

[1] Émile Durkheim, *Education and Sociology,* translated by D. F. Pocock, London, Cohen and West; Glencoe, Free Press, 1956.
[2] Émile Durkheim, *Moral Education,* translated by Everett K. Wilson and Herman Schnurer, Glencoe, Free Press, 1961.

[3] Émile Durkheim, *The Evolution of Educational Thought,* translated by Peter Collins, Boston, and London, Routledge and Kegan Paul, 1977.

[4] Steven Lukes, *Émile Durkheim: His Life and Work,* London, Penguin, 1975.

Bibliography of Durkheim's Major Works

ORIGINAL WORKS

(Durkheim's books, including those which appeared post-humously, were first published in Paris by Felix Alcan, unless otherwise stated.)

1893 *De la division du travail social: étude sur l'organisation des sociétés supérieures.*

1895 *Les règles de la méthode sociologique.*

1897 *Le suicide: étude de sociologie.*

1903 (with Marcel Mauss) 'De quelques formes primitives de classification: contribution a l'étude des représentations collectives', *L'Année sociologique,* vol. 6, pp. 1-72.

1912 *Les formes élémentaires de la vie religieuse: le système totémique en Australie.*

Published posthumously

1922 *Education et sociologie.* Introduction by Paul Fauconnet.

1924 *Sociologie et philosophie.* Preface by Celestin Bouglé.

1925 *L'Education morale.* Foreword by P. Fauconnet.

1928 *Le socialisme: sa définition, ses débuts, la doctrine Saint-Simonienne.* Introduction by Marcel Mauss, Paris, Presses Universitaires de France.

1938 *L'Evolution pédagogique en France.* Introduction by Maurice Halbwachs; two volumes.

1950 *Leçons de sociologie: physique des moeurs et du droit.* Foreword by H. Nail Kubali; introduction by Georges Davy, Istanbul, L'université d'Istanbul, and Paris, Presses Universitaires de France.

1955 *Pragmatisme et sociologie.* Reconstructed from students' notes by Armand Cuvillier, Paris, Vrin.

ENGLISH TRANSLATIONS

(Dates are those of hardback editions, whereas references in text include paperback edns.)

1915 *The Elementary Forms of the Religious Life: a Study in Religious Sociology.* Trans. Joseph Ward Swain, London: Allen & Unwin; New York: Macmillan.

1933 *The Division of Labour in Society.* Trans. with an introduction by George Simpson, New York: Macmillan.

1938 *The Rules of Sociological Method.* Trans. Sarah A. Solovay and John H. Mueller; introduction by Goerge E. G. Catlin, Chicago: University of Chicago Press.

1951 *Suicide: a Study in Sociology.* Trans. John A. Spaulding and George Simpson; introduction by George Simpson, Glencoe: Free Press; London: Routledge & Paul, 1952.

1953 *Sociology and Philosophy.* Trans. D. F. Pocock; introduction by J. G. Peristiany, London: Cohen & West; Glencoe: Free Press.

1956 *Education and Sociology.* Trans. with an introduction by Sherwood D. Fox; Foreword by Talcot Parsons, Glencoe: Free Press.

1957 *Professional Ethics and Civic Morals.* Translation of *Leçons de Sociologie* by Cornelia Brookfield, London: Routledge & Kegan Paul.

1958 *Socialism and Saint-Simon* (subsequently entitled *Socialism*). Trans. Charlotte Sattler; introduction by Alvin W. Gouldner, Yellow Springs: Antioch Press; London: Routledge & Kegan Paul, 1959.

1960 *Montesquieu and Rousseau.* Trans. Ralph Manheim, Ann Arbor: University of Michigan Press.

1961 *Moral Education: a Study in the Theory and Application of the Sociology of Education.* Trans. Everett K. Wilson and Herman

Schnurer; introduction by Everett K. Wilson, Glencoe: Free Press.

1963 *Primitive Classification*. Trans. with an introduction by Rodney Needham, London: Cohen & West; Chicago: University of Chicago Press.

1977 *The Evolution of Educational Thought*. Trans. Peter Collins, London: Routledge & Kegan Paul.

ESSAYS AND REVIEWS

Bellah, Robert N. (ed.) *Émile Durkheim on Morality and Society,* Chicago, University of Chicago Press, 1973.

Duvignaud, Jean (ed.) *Journal Sociologique,* Paris, Presses Universitaires de France, 1969.

Nandon, Yash (ed.) *Émile Durkheim; Contributions to L'Année Sociologique,* London, Collier-Macmillan, New York, Free Press, 1980.

Filloux, Jean-Claude (ed.), Émile Durkheim, *La Science Sociale et l'Action,* Paris, Presses Universitaires de France, 1970.

Traugott, Mark (ed.) *Émile Durkheim on Institutional Analysis,* Chicago, University of Chicago Press, 1978.

Annotated Bibliography of Secondary sources

1. GENERAL

Harry Alpert, *Emile Durkheim and His Sociology,* New York, Columbia University Press, 1939. This was one of the first books in English on Durkheim, and it was very influential in making his sociology palatable to American sociologists.

Anthony Giddens, *Durkheim,* London, Fontana Modern Masters, 1978. A very brief but extremely perceptive outline of some of the main aspects of Durkheim's thought.

Steven Lukes, *Emile Durkheim: His Life and Work,* London, Allen Lane, 1973; Penguin Peregrine paperback, 1975. The most authoritative and magisterial intellectual biography of Durkheim. An essential reference book.

Dominick La Capra, *Emile Durkheim, Sociologist and Philosopher,* Ithaca, New York, Cornell University Press, 1972. A very philosophical treatment of Durkheim's thought; sometimes illuminating, at other times more La Capra than Durkheim, but always stimulating.

Talcott Parsons, *The Structure of Social Action,* New York, McGraw-Hill, 1937, and The Free Press 1949, chs. 8-12. Parsons was the dominant theorist in American sociology in its period of expansion after the Second World War. His treatment of Durkheim in this work was in terms of a convergence with other theorists, such as Weber and Pareto, leading towards Parsons' own voluntaristic theory of social action. It entailed postulating a "break" in Durkheim's thought, after *Suicide,* when it turned from postivism towards voluntarism, i.e. emphasizing values (although Parsons objected that Durkheim had "overshot the mark and gone clean into idealism" because he did not give attention to individual will and effort). Despite the criticisms that can be made against this interpretation, there is no doubt that Parsons firmly established Durkheim's reputation as one of the two great founding theorists of modern sociology (along with Weber).

Talcott Parsons, "Emile Durkheim" in *International Encyclopedia of the Social Sciences,* New York, Macmillan, 1968, vol. 4, pp. 311-20. This much later account of Durkheim's sociology provides a fascinating contrast with the earlier treatment by Parsons. It reflects many of the changes that had taken place in sociological theory over the thirty-year period.

Edward A. Tiryakian "Emile Durkheim" in Tom Bottomore and Robert Nisbet (eds.), *A History of Sociological Analysis,* London, Heinemann, New York, Basic Books, pp. 187-236, 1978. This imaginative appaisal of Durkheim's thought reflects some of the recent developments in Durkheimian studies.

Kurt H. Wolff, (ed.) *Emile Durkheim 1858-1917,* Ohio, Ohio State University Press, 1960; republished as Emile Durkheim *et al, Essays on Sociology and Philosophy,* New York, Harper Torchbooks, 1964. An important collection of essays on various aspects of Durkheim's life and work.

2. DIVISION OF LABOUR

J. A. Barnes, "Durkheim's *Division of Labour in Society*", in *Man,* 2, (June 1966), pp. 158-75. A critical review of Durkheim's Division of Labour thesis and a discussion of relevant evidence.

Leon Sheleff, "From Restitutive Law to Repressive Law: Durkheim's *The Division of Labour in Society* revisited" *European Journal of Sociology,* 16, 1, 1975, pp. 16-45. Another critical review and a consideration of various suggested modifications to Durkheim's thesis.

3. METHODOLOGY AND EPISTEMOLOGY

Paul Q. Hirst, *Durkheim, Bernard and Epistemology*, London and Boston, Routledge & Kegan Paul, 1975. This is a penetrating, if somewhat hyper-critical, analysis of Durkheim's epistemology as found in *The Rules of Sociological Method*. Hirst acknowledges the importance of Durkheim's attempt to give sociology a scientific basis, but judges it a failure. The judgement is too harsh, and does not sufficiently take account of Durkheim's works other than *The Rules*. Nor need faults in epistemology cancel out virtuous results.

4. SUICIDE

Whitney Pope, *Durkheim's Suicide: A Classic Analyzed*, Chicago, University of Chicago Press, 1976. The best full-length treatment of *Suicide*.

Anthony Giddens, *The Sociology of Suicide: A selection of Readings*, London, Frank Cass, 1971. This includes Gidden's own article on the debate about suicide in nineteenth-century France.

J. D. Douglas, *The Social Meanings of Suicide*, Princeton, Princeton University Press, 1967. A critique of Durkheim's approach, and an advocacy of a more phenomenological approach.

5. RELIGION AND SOCIOLOGY OF KNOWLEDGE

Mary Douglas, *Natural Symbols*, London, Barrie & Rockliff, 1970 and Penguin 1973. This, and other works by Douglas, provide an example of various developments of Durkheim's ideas on symbols and rituals in society.

W. S. F. Pickering, (ed.), *Durkheim on Religion*, London and Boston, Routledge & Kegan Paul, 1975. Selections from Durkheim's writings on religion are included along with some of the early criticisms of his work in this field.

Talcott Parsons, "Durkheim on Religion Revisited" in Charles Y. Glock & P. E. Hammond (eds.), 1973, *Beyond the Classics? Essays in the Scientific Study of Religion*, New York, Harper, 1973, pp. 156-180. Fascinating for its insights into the ever-changing nature of Parsons' own sociology as much as for its insights into the possibilities of Durkheim's ideas being developed and applied.

Peter M. Worsely, "Emile Durkheim's Theory of Knowledge", *Sociological Review*, 4, 1, 1956, pp. 47-62. A classic appraisal of Durkheim's sociology of knowledge.

6. POLITICS

Tom Bottomore, "A Marxist Consideration of Durkheim", *Social Forces*, **59**, 4, 1981, pp. 902-17. A critique of Durkheim's sociology from a conventional Marxist viewpoint; thorough, but disappointing on imaginative effort to see how Durkheim's sociology might yield useful complementary insights to Marx's.

Jean-Claude Filloux, *Durkheim et le socialisme*, Geneva and Paris, Librairie Droz, 1977. An excellent account of Durkheim's political ideas and thier relevance for democratic socialism.

Anthony Giddens, "Durkheim's Political Sociology", *Sociological Review*, **19**, 4, 1971, pp. 477-519. This was an important re-appraisal of Durkheim's political sociology.

Jeffrey Prager, "Moral Integration and Political Inclusion: A Comparison of Durkheim's and Weber's Theories of Democracy", *Social Forces*, **59**, 4, 1981, pp. 918-50. This is typical of recent appreciations of Durkheim's political sociology and its relevance for issues of democracy.

7. EDUCATION AND MORALS

Basil Bernstein, "Class and Pedagogies: Visible and Invisible", in Jerome Karabel & A. H. Halsey (eds.), *Power and Ideology in Education*, New York and London, Oxford University Press, 1977, pp. 511-34. An elaboration and application of Durkheim's ideas on education and types of social solidarity — mechanical and organic — in relation to classes, social reproduction, and symbolic control. This volume also contains excerpts from Durkheim's works on education and appreciative evaluations of their continuing usefulness.

Mohamed Cherkaoui, "Consensus or Conflict? Return to Durkheim's Proteiform Theory", in *Theory and Society*, **10**, 1, 1981, pp. 127-38. Makes the case for seeing conflict as the category at the centre of Durkheim's theory of educational systems.

Ernest Wallwork, *Durkheim: Morality and Milieu*, Cambridge, Mass., Harvard University Press, 1972. Comprehensive treatment of Durkheim's sociology of morals and education.

8. MISCELLANEOUS

Philippe Besnard, "La formation de l'equipe de l'Année sociologique" in *Revue francaise de sociologie*, **20**, 1978, pp. 7-31. An extremely detailed and well-researched account of the formation of the team of scholars involved in collaboration with Durkheim on *L'Année sociologique*.

Terry N. Clark, *Prophets and Patrons: The French University and the Emergence of the Social Sciences,* Cambridge, Harvard University Press, 1973. Useful discussion of the institutional setting of Durkheim and *L'Année sociologique* group.

Etudes durkheimiennes, Bulletin d'information, prepared by the Groupe d'études durkheimiennes, Foundation Maison des Sciences de l'Homme, 54 bd. Raspail, 75270 Paris, France.

Index